® **teach yourself**

games programming

alan thorn

for over 60 years, more than 50
million people have learnt over 750
subjects the **teach yourself** way,
with impressive results.

be where you want to be
with **teach yourself**

For UK order enquiries: please contact Bookpoint Ltd, 130 Milton Park, Abingdon, Oxon OX14 4SB. Telephone: +44 (0)1235 827720. Fax: +44 (0)1235 400454. Lines are open 09.00–17.00, Monday to Saturday, with a 24-hour message answering service. Details about our titles and how to order are available at www.teachyourself.co.uk.

For USA order enquiries: please contact McGraw-Hill Customer Services, PO Box 545, Blacklick, OH 43004-0545, USA. Telephone: 1-800-722-4726. Fax: 1-614-755-5645.

For Canada order enquiries: please contact McGraw-Hill Ryerson Ltd, 300 Water St, Whitby, Ontario L1N 9B6, Canada. Telephone: 905 430 5000. Fax: 905 430 5020.

Long renowned as the authoritative source for self-guided learning – with more than 50 million copies sold worldwide – the **teach yourself** series includes over 500 titles in the fields of languages, crafts, hobbies, business, computing and education.

British Library Cataloguing in Publication Data: a catalogue record for this title is available from The British Library.

Library of Congress Catalog Card Number: on file.

First published in UK 2007 by Hodder Education, 338 Euston Road, London NW1 3BH.

First published in US 2007 by The McGraw-Hill Companies, Inc.

The **teach yourself** name is a registered trademark of Hodder Headline.

Computer hardware and software brand names mentioned in this book are protected by their respective trademarks and are acknowledged.

Typeset by MacDesign, Southampton

Printed in Great Britain for Hodder Education, a division of Hodder Headline, an Hachette Livre UK Company, 338 Euston Road, London NW1 3BH, by Cox & Wyman Ltd, Reading, Berkshire.

The publisher has used its best endeavours to ensure that the URLs for external websites referred to in this book are correct and active at the time of going to press. However, the publisher and the author have no responsibility for the websites and can make no guarantee that a site will remain live or that the content will remain relevant, decent or appropriate.

Hodder Headline's policy is to use papers that are natural, renewable and recyclable products and made from wood grown in sustainable forests. The logging and manufacturing processes are expected to conform to the environmental regulations of the country of origin.

Impression number   10 9 8 7 6 5 4 3 2 1   3602 5152   12/07

Year   2011 2010 2009 2008 2007

contents

The code companion for this book can be found at:
http://www.alanthorn.net/TYGPCode.zip

introduction

What exactly are computer games? And how on earth does somebody go about making one? Perhaps you're looking to establish your own business making games, or maybe you want to get a job in the industry, or maybe you're just plain curious. Hopefully, this book will answer your questions.

Quite a number of years ago, when I wanted to learn how games were made, there weren't any books around on the subject to learn from. I didn't know anybody who made games, and none of my family or friends really had much of an idea about how computers worked. During my early teens I played a lot of games and as I approached 15 I decided I'd had enough of just playing, and now it was about time I actually tried making a game. So I abandoned my Sega Mega Drive (Genesis) console and I opted to buy a shiny new 486 PC. It was bigger than my TV. In the bookshops I searched for something, anything, that told me how to make games. I noticed there were lots of formal technical manuals. These were long boring programming references, and the DIY PC titles that are now so common were just beginning to emerge along with dial-up Internet. But there were no game books. Though I didn't know at the time, the information I needed was all there, it just wasn't integrated in one book in the context of games. As a result, I learned games programming the hard way. Along with this I also learned that no matter how fast I can take in all this information, the speed of technology is much, much faster. So I came to understand that no matter how much I thought I knew, there were always more things to learn. In fact, learning how to make games taught me lots of other things. In order to make a racing game with realistic car actions and collisions I needed to learn physics, and to simulate the physical reactions properly I also needed to learn maths. In time I became quite surprised at exactly how demanding games programming was, about how much a person needed to know and the whole range of subjects game development encompassed.

Today, game development is simpler than it once was and it's getting even simpler, thanks to the hard groundwork laid by many people. This is substantiated by the vast rise of new development startups around the globe. Individuals, small teams and large teams all ready to make games and show the gaming public what they have to offer. Part of this increase in game developers is because technology has become more accessible to people with all budgets, and it's also because information is more readily available and simpler to understand. This book aims to be among this new kind of Teach Yourself books, which offer a human look at sometimes intimidating subjects. It's mainly aimed at confident PC users with some previous programming experience, preferably in C++. But everybody is welcome to try. It's a book you can follow at your own pace. In short, this book is written to be exactly the kind of thing I wish I'd had available to me back then when I wanted to learn games programming. Since then, I've made a lot of mistakes, asked lots of silly questions and generally made plenty of mess-ups. But I've learned an awful lot from those mistakes and, if I'm to be honest, it's taught me lots more than a university ever did. For this reason I've put together this book on games programming to help others learn how games are made and how to get started at making games themselves. Hopefully, along the way, you will learn lots of other things too.

Alan Thorn

2007

01 computer games

In this chapter you will learn about:

- game genres
- gaming devices
- famous games
- preparing to make games

Science may set limits to knowledge, but should not set limits to imagination.

Bertrand Russell

1.1 Computer games

The power and influence of video games cannot be understated, both for business and for the millions who play them every year. Over time, video games have been called an industry, an art and a science. But whatever the truth of those claims, video games have already entrenched a number of colourful characters into our psyche and popular culture. Characters we take for granted, like the blazing blue Sonic the Hedgehog, the overalls-wearing Luigi and Mario, and the shapely Lara Croft, to name just a few of them. However, unlike film and music, with their own network of celebrity culture, the details about how games are made and who make them remain unknown to most people. How are games made? This book aims to answer that exciting question. It aims to lift the lid on games and show you how to make your own. It explores the creation of two different games, specially made for this book, working through from beginning to end, and covering a range of games programming topics along the way. This chapter begins our journey, by first looking at the history of games in comparison with the industry today. It also takes a brief look at some of the interesting things to come later.

Computer games are a comparatively new invention. They came into being because people wanted to do fun things on the computer in their spare time, and, given the human fondness for fun, games were inevitable once the first computer was manufactured. The first recorded game was made in 1948, and began as a missile simulation for the US military. Games such as *Noughts and Crosses*, *SpaceWar* and *John's Great Adventure* followed in the 1950s and 1960s. By the 1970s and 1980s, computer games had evolved into a fully-fledged industry, beginning with arcade games and these eventually migrated into the home via PCs (personal computers) and gaming consoles. This leads us to the computer games of today, which – for better or worse – are a product of this legacy, mixed with the interests of big business. Indeed, they have at various stages come to be a revolution more profitable than the music industry.

The computer that games are played on can take various forms, and it has changed widely over the years in line with technology. Computer games have consistently featured on the PC throughout their history, and they've also featured on dedicated home systems called gaming consoles. Examples of these (at the time of writing) are Xbox 360, PS3 and Nintendo Wii (or Revolution). The distinction between a PC and gaming console has also led to a distinction in terms. 'Computer games' refers to PC games, while 'video games' identifies those on consoles. But the distinction is largely academic, especially since the same game can feature on many different platforms. Therefore, this book will use the term 'computer game' to refer to games on both PC and consoles except where otherwise stated. Games also feature on other platforms, such as mobile phones, portable hand-held devices, and even certain cable TV packages.

1.2 Games in practice

Ever since the 1980s, gaming has saturated the world with a variety of franchises and characters; some loved and some hated. Games have also touched, and still touch, the realms of ethics and philosophy. Some parents have campaigned to censor various games and the industry generally, calling them dangerous to the ethics of modern culture. Much of this has been a reactionary movement towards the violence in games, and the influence it is said to have. Recently, there was much controversy over Australia banning *Grand Theft Auto: San Andreas* from stores by refusing classification due to hidden sex scenes. But this just proved again that people, when told they cannot have something, tend to desire it even more. Censorship, controversy, classifications and banning have been secret weapons for the commercial successes of many games, including: *Night Trap*, *Phantasmagoria*, *Zombie Smashers X2*, *Doom* and *Grand Theft Auto*.

Games did not begin with such controversy surrounding them. They were originally seen to be innocent; made for nerds by nerds, and the production of early games was a solo or small team affair. On early systems like Spectrum ZX and Commodore 64, games were distributed on cassette tapes. They needed to be forwarded and rewound just like normal tapes. However, these humble beginnings gave way to big business. And now, games have followed technology to deliver multi-million dollar investments onto PCs and consoles. The transition from small business to big business, however, was a gradual one. In the interim, some of the most famous games emerged. These included: *Tetris*, *Space Invaders*, *Pac Man* and *Donkey Kong*. *Donkey Kong* is particularly significant because it featured the debut of later gaming hero, Super Mario. He would later become the main character in Nintendo's franchise *Super Mario Brothers*. Mario was to become a mascot for Nintendo and their 8-bit and 16-bit platforms, the NES and Super Nintendo. The competitive Sega also sought to find identity in the form of a gaming mascot, one which would become equally as famous. This character was to be Sonic the Hedgehog. In an interesting response to Sonic, the Amiga platform (a rival) sported a similar mascot known as Zool. However, though popular, it never gained the notoriety of Sonic or Mario. Character franchises were nothing new to computer games, though. Before Mario, Sonic and Zool, there were a host of others including: Dizzy, Punchy and Wonderboy – none of whom exist in modern gaming. Now, the marketing of games is less character-based and more focused on serial blockbusters like the movie industry. There are perhaps only a handful of exceptions to this. For example, one of the most notable characters to be born from modern gaming is Lara Croft. The world of gaming might have changed, but the culture of historical gaming still lives on, known as a Retro Gaming. This is itself still an industry, with its own magazine (*Retro Gamer*) and a number of websites, such as **theoldcomputer.com**.

Emulators

Retro games are played using emulator software. These programs run on modern PCs and simulate older computers. There is a NES and Super Nintendo emulator, a Sega Master System and Megadrive emulator, a Commodore Amiga and Commodore 64 emulator, and lots more. Each emulator plays their respective games through a series of files called ROM images, and there is usually one ROM image for each game. To learn more about retro games, try searching for "emulators" on Google, or another search engine.

1.3 Gaming genres

Genres define categories, and in modern gaming there are many types of games. Each computer game appears under the umbrella of a genre. Some games are typical of a specific genre, some are a mixture of genres, and some are innovators of new genres. The genre describes the kind of game you can expect to play, its content, the subject matter and the style. Just like movies, they can be horror, action, adventure, etc. But computer games also have genres unique to them. These describe the way a game is played, e.g. one that involves jumping from platform to platform is in the genre of 'platform game'. Similarly, a game about battling armies is termed a 'strategy game'. The following sections examine some of the most common genres.

Platform game

Perhaps the most famous conception of computer games are those of the classic platform games (platformers). It's an image which goes hand-in-hand with that of teenage boys crossed-legged in front of the computer, pressing frantically at a controller. Platformers started their life in 2D and later migrated to 3D where most of them remain. Their characterizing feature is a series of platforms, cliffs or ledges suspended in the air across which a character must travel, fighting baddies, avoiding obstacles and collecting items in order to complete the level. Some of the most famous platform games have acquired cult status in popular culture. These are games like: *Super Mario Brothers*, *Sonic The Hedgehog*, *Earthworm Jim*, *Jazz Jackrabbit* and *Psychonauts*.

Beat 'em up

Beat 'em ups, otherwise known as 'scroll fighters' or 'brawlers', include old arcade classics like *Final Fight*, or games like *Streets of Rage*, *Punisher* or *Zombie Smashers X2*. The beat 'em up is a genre where characters walk streets, clubs and other venues beating up almost everybody they encounter. The beat 'em up was controversial because, like shoot 'em ups, the main aims of the game were based on violence.

First-person shooter (FPS)

Arguably the most successful genre of game, first-person shooters are typically violent. Viewed from first-person perspectives the ultimate aim is to shoot other characters or objects. Famous games of this genre include: *Doom*, *Quake*, *Unreal Tournament* and the *Half Life* series. This genre began with *Wolfenstein*, by ID Software. Since then, FPS games have become controversial since most feature blood, gore, and sometimes sexual content. A variation is the third-person shooter, which is the same style of game, but from a different viewpoint.

Strategy and realtime strategy (RTS)

Strategy games are a diverse genre divided into two types; turn-based and realtime. The genre itself immerses the player into an authoritative role, commanding an army or nation. It involves resource-gathering, base-building and tactical operations. The subtle difference between turn-based and realtime is implied by their names. Turn-based variants, like *Heroes of Might and Magic* or *The Battle for Wesnoth*, feature competing factions that take turns in moving their armies and gathering wealth. Realtime games, on the other hand, are more action-orientated and opponents work simultaneously. Famous RTS games include: *Starcraft*, *Command & Conquer* and *Dark Reign*.

Role-playing game (RPG)

One of the largest genres, an RPG is based on pen-and-paper ancestors like *Dungeons and Dragons*. RPGs are usually set in fantasy medieval worlds with wizards and dragons, and encourage gamers to live as a character, choosing their appearance, developing skills, and participating in the world. They usually involve quests, battles and other story-related challenges. Some of the most notable games in this genre are: *Oblivion*, *Everquest*, *World of Warcraft* and *Dink Smallwood*.

Adventure games

Adventure games are one of the victims of commercial gaming. It is a genre which has been neglected over the past few years. This is mainly because such games are associated with commercial failure. Adventure games are typically not action-based, and instead rely on story and object-based puzzles. Famous adventures include: *Myst*, *Day of the Tentacle*, *Tex Murphy*, *Monkey Island* and *Grim Fandango*.

Sports games

Most of these are franchises associated with official sporting leagues. Many are produced by giant publisher Electronic Arts. Games include *FIFA International Soccer* and *NHL Ice Hockey*. Sports games are not usually the biggest sellers, except when they coincide with sporting events like the World Cup.

Simulations

Simulation or sim games are also called 'games of status' or 'mixed game'. A simulation replicates a real-world system on the computer. A space shuttle simulation, for example, is programmed to incorporate astro-physics to assess how the shuttle would react if these conditions were re-created in real life. It's a virtual system on the computer. Though computer game simulations are based on the idea of a real-world scenario, they're often exaggerated or simplified by poetic licence to make things more fun. Typically, a sim game involves a combination of chance, skill and strategy. In them, a gamer may take command over armies, or businesses or some other real-world aspect of life. One of the most famous sim games was developed by Maxis, and is called *Sim City*, and its sequel was *Sim City 2000*. In these games, the player finds themselves making financial, social and building decisions about the construction of a metropolis. Other famous sims include: *The Sims*, *Theme Park*, *Theme Hospital*, *Rollercoaster Tycoon* and *Teenage Lawnmower*.

Casual games

Casual games are an interesting genre that has increased in number and variety with the expansion of the Internet, and are typified by their general mass appeal. Easy to learn, requiring no specific gamer skills or experience, they are usually played online or downloaded from the Net. They include fun games like: *Solitaire*, *Chess* and other board games, *Samorost* and many more. They're the kind of games you can play in an office over lunch, or at home when you're not in the mood for much intense action. These sorts of games have not only increased in popularity, but are also cheap to produce.

1.4 Gaming devices

Keyboard and mouse

A keyboard is the oldest control existing today, closely followed by a mouse. Both of these are the hallmark controls of a PC, though a number of modern consoles, like the Playstation, have support for keyboards that can plug in and work for selected games. The keyboard and mouse are some of the simplest controls to use, partly because gamers and society are so accustomed to them, either through work or at home.

Joystick

Joysticks began in aviation control, and now the movable stick is often used for games. It became famous with arcade games, and then migrated to home consoles and PCs. Most still offer support for them, and a wide variety of games can be controlled using joysticks. On the PC, joysticks can also be used as an alternative pointing device for a mouse, often for users with disabilities like cerebral palsy or motor neurone disease.

Game pad

The most popular choice of controller for modern consoles is the control pad, or game pad. This is a flat hand-held device with a directional arrow pad and buttons – an abbreviated keyboard containing only buttons relevant to games. Game pads have become the standard control device among consoles, and for this reason most are shipped with at least one game pad.

Eye Toy

In 2003 the Eye Toy controller was released for the Playstation 2 and PSP (Playstation Portable). Essentially, it's similar to a standard web cam (web camera) like those featured on a PC. but, its light-sensitivity allows players to control games via their own body movements when standing in front of the camera. A whole variety of games were released specifically for the Eye Toy controller, including a number of dance games.

Dance pad

One of the most popular and recent innovations in game controllers is the dance pad, a floor mat featuring flat blocks and buttons large enough to be stepped on. The mat can also be used as a substitute control pad, but it is mostly used for dance games. These games work by demanding gamers step on certain buttons in time to music and at challenging, calorie-burning speeds.

Light gun

An obsolete controller, partly due to technical issues relating to new kinds of screens and monitors. The light gun used to be a popular device on 8-Bit and 16-Bit consoles like the NES and MegaDrive. This device was a plastic gun that could be shot at the screen and software could detect where the shot would hit. A wide variety of shooting games were played with this very specific gun controller.

1.5 Famous games

Throughout gaming history there have been possibly hundreds of thousands of games released. Among this number some have been more notable than others. Usually this was because they were genre defining, or commercially successful, or both.

Pac-Man

This was created in 1979 and became a hit upon release. It's almost synonymous with computer games, and is still released on the latest consoles like the Xbox 360. Its objective is simple. Each level is a maze and the player's objective is to guide Pac-Man safely through, eating gold coins along the way. A level is complete when all coins have been eaten. The levels are littered with enemies trying to catch Pac-Man. Like many games from the time, a player starts with three lives and can earn extra ones. It ends if Pac-Man dies and there are no lives left.

Lemmings

In August 1989 Mike Dailly wanted to see how small (in terms of pixels) a game character could be on screen before a game became unplayable. This experiment led to the creation of one of the most famous games, *Lemmings*. The game was refreshingly new for its time. Instead of controlling a character, players were in command of skills; like builder, blocker, digger, etc. The aim of each level was to guide a family of lemmings home safely. The levels were themselves a big puzzle, featuring all kinds of dangers. The player's task was to plan how the lemmings could get home, by managing skills. Some lemmings could become diggers and tunnel holes to avoid overland threats, others could become builders to climb over dangerous terrain.

Doom

Doom was a first-person shooter game, largely developed by John Carmack in 1993. The main objective was to survive each level, finding the exit and shooting baddies. It became famous partly due to its controversial violence, but also because of its 3D graphics. Furthermore, *Doom* featured designable levels and could be run multiplayer over a network. Since then, many FPS games have been called Doom clones.

Sonic and Mario

Sonic and *Mario* were originally platformers, but have since generated many spin-offs of different genres. The two characters have become part of popular culture and people across the world recognize their pictures. The commercial success of both franchises led to many platform clones during the 1980s and 1990s.

World of Warcraft

This MMORPG (Massively Multiplayer Online Role-Playing Game) is the latest controversial video game. *World of Warcraft* (WoW) is a subscription-based game where players create a character and live in a virtual world with other players across the globe. It is probably the most successful of its type, with around 8 million players. WoW has been criticized by psychologists who are worried about the addiction levels amongst its players.

1.6 Preparing to make games

The games industry is an exciting place to be right now because there's such diversity, and because nobody is exactly certain what to expect next. This book is mainly about how to make games and is aimed at people looking to get started in the industry, or to make games as a hobby. Much of the rest of this book will oversee the creation of two different games, using different tools and techniques. By the end of this book, readers should have a good understanding of the fundamentals of game-making.

Game 1: Sokoban

Sokoban is the famous Japanese box pushing puzzle game. The player controls a warehouse keeper, and each level is a different maze. The objective is to push a series of boxes through the maze and onto destination squares. A level is complete when all the destination squares have boxes on them. The keeper cannot pull boxes, and they cannot push more than one box together. Only one box can be pushed at once. It's simple to play but difficult to master, as we'll see in the next chapter.

Game 2: Hex

Hex is a two-player strategy game set on a hex grid (board). The board can be different sizes, but this book will consider a 7×7 board. Each player takes a different colour, and they take turns in putting a piece on the board in any vacant space. The objective is to build a connected path between two opposite sides of the board. One player tries to connect left to right, and the other tries to connect top to bottom. The winner is the first player to connect the opposite sides. We will examine how to create artificial intelligence for this puzzle. This means we will make the computer reason about its moves so it can play against the player.

Development overview

It is recommended the book is read in sequential order. The following summarizes each chapter and the subjects they will cover.

Chapter 2: Design concentrates on designing Sokoban. It defines the objective and rules, what the player can and cannot do.

It also introduces design issues encountered in computer games, and explains how Sokoban will be developed.

Chapter 3: Programming introduces two IDEs (integrated development environments) for making games. It also explains some of the basics of games programming, applicable to almost all games. This book assumes some familiarity with C++, though code samples are explained.

Chapter 4: Graphics programming looks at graphics programming in C++ for Sokoban. It explores graphics generally, and explains how developers draw fast-paced graphics to the screen.

Chapter 5: Audio programming explores the intricacies of music and sound for games. We will examine how to play common audio files like MP3, WAV and OGG.

Chapter 6: Game mechanics brings graphics and sound together and completes the first game, Sokoban.

Chapter 7: Web games introduces the second game, Hex. This will be a web game – one that can be played in a web page. To make this game, Adobe Director will be used.

Chapter 8: Artificial intelligence aims to answer the question 'How can the computer think and make moves?' To complete Hex, the brains behind the computer opponent need to be made.

Chapter 9: Distribution and support explains how to build installation programs and provide support via online forums.

Chapter 10: Action effects and techniques takes a tour of techniques used in making modern games. It looks at features like collision detection, culling and Z-ordering.

Chapter 11: Designing Action-Bot pulls together the work from Chapter 10 and applies it by designing an end of level boss for a hypothetical action game.

Chapter 12: The games industry considers how to get a job in the games industry, how to start a business making games, and explores some of the challenges which face the games industry.

Summary

In this chapter some important topics were introduced. In addition to looking at the history of computer games, it also outlined the path the book will take.

02

design

In this chapter you will learn about:

- the nature and rules of Sokoban
- tile-based games
- graphics and sound libraries
- gaming platforms

Software gets slower faster than hardware gets faster.

Wirth's Law

2.1 Defining Sokoban

The game development process begins with design, that is, by considering what we are to make. To do this, we need to ask questions. What will the game be about? What is the objective? What kinds of things will the game include? All of these questions must be answered during design. It is to this subject, therefore, that we now turn.

When a lone developer or a team resolve to make a game, one of the first things they do is brainstorm about the kind of game. Further to this, they will raise ideas about the sorts of features to include; the characters, the setting, the story and so on. In this case, a puzzle game called *Sokoban* is going to be created. Sokoban is a Japanese word intended to conjure up the idea of a warehouse keeper. (One of the first video games based on Sokoban was a Sega Megadrive implementation called *Shove It! The Warehouse Game*.) The player views the game from above in a bird's eye view. They control a warehouse keeper in a maze, and the mission on each level is to push crates onto designated spots. They can't pull the crates, and nor can they push several together – only *one* crate can be *pushed* at a time. It seems simple enough to play at first, but it is deceptively difficult. Some of the first levels are easy and they become progressively trickier, with some of the hardest levels seeming almost impossible to solve. In fact, it's not unheard of for people having to spend several days or weeks attempting to solve a specific level. Figure 2.1 demonstrates a sample Sokoban layout, one of many.

The history of Sokoban

Sokoban was first developed in 1980 by Hiroyuki Imabayashi, and since then many versions of this game have been created. The Web is replete with different implementations, some commercial and others free. A quick search on Google will reveal lots of websites featuring Sokoban puzzles to try freely, and its general prevalence worldwide is what makes it such a good place to begin game programming.

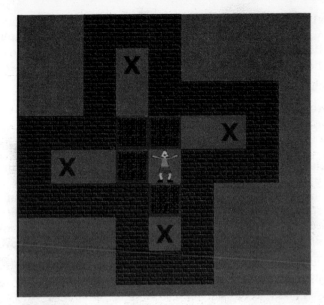

Figure 2.1 A sample Sokoban layout

Formal rules

Most GDDs (Game Design Documents) contain a formal defini-tion of the rules of a game. The purpose of this is to list the rules, explaining what they mean, to ensure no confusion will arise throughout development. What exactly, for example, is a level? What can they contain? And what does it mean to win a level, and what does it mean to lose? For Sokoban, the funda-mentals can be thought of as follows.

1   A single **level** represents one Sokoban puzzle. An entire game will typically consist of many levels presented to the player in a sequential fashion. When one level is completed, the player can move on to the next one, and so on. In any Sokoban level there will be the player, any boxes to be pushed, usually some walls arranged like a maze to make the puzzle difficult, and finally the destination squares, which are places where the boxes must be pushed.

2   The **objective** of a level is to push all the available boxes onto the destination squares. In any level there are usually as many boxes as there are destination squares, so there should be no spare boxes remaining when the level is completed.

3 A **move** is the process of pushing a box or moving the player, without a box, to another square. However, when a move does involve a box there are several rules governing how a box can be moved.

(a) A box can be pushed.

(b) A box cannot be pulled.

(c) Only one box at a time can pushed. If, for example, there are two side by side, they cannot both be pushed together.

4 A level is **won** when all the destination squares are occupied by boxes. Though there are usually no spare boxes, the important point is that there must be no vacant destination squares. The level can be **lost** if it becomes impossible to continue. For example, a box could be pushed into a corner and since the player cannot pull boxes, it can never be moved.

Variations. There are some versions of Sokoban that count the number of moves the player makes, in terms of how many box pushes they perform in a single level. Some variations even specify a minimum limit so a level can only be completed provided the boxes reach their destination in a minimum number of pushes. The Sokoban we shall be making here, however, will not make this requirement.

2.2 Sokoban and perspectives

A level is the playing area of Sokoban and there are potentially many arrangements it can be in, some of which are explored shortly. There are several ways a level could be presented to a player: tile-based, isometric and even a 3D layout where the player can zoom in and out and look around at the puzzle from all angles. The developer needs to decide how the game ought to be shown; something that is both fun to use and suitable for its needs. The following three perspectives are the most common to be found in modern gaming.

Isometric

One of the oldest and most prolific perspectives in gaming is the isometric view. Its aim is to show a 3D-like world in 2D. It takes a game level, and divides it into a grid with cells of equal size.

The camera is then set to a fixed position so that all the objects appear to be facing you at an angle of 45 degrees. Imagine standing inside a cube. The viewer is placed at the top-right corner and faces the opposite bottom left corner, as though looking diagonally downwards to the floor. Though an isometric perspective (see Figure 2.2) is interesting and has been used for Sokoban games, it will not be used for our version.

Figure 2.2 Ultima Online, an example of isometric view

3D perspective

3D games let the player control a camera and wander around (see Figure 2.3). In this perspective, it's possible to see the game objects from different angles, and gamers can explore the environment in a more intimate – though sometimes seasick – way. There have been a number of 3D Sokoban games, but we will not be using this either for our version.

Tile-based top-down view

The ideal perspective for Sokoban is the top-down view (see Figure 2.4). In this way, the entire layout of the level can be seen at once and the player is shown everything they need to know in order to solve the puzzle. Furthermore, this perspective is simple to use. For this reason it is commonly found in computer games. This will be the perspective for our Sokoban.

Figure 2.3 Half-Life 2, an example of a 3D perspective view

Figure 2.4 Legend of Zelda, showing a top-down view

2.3 Sokoban and tile-based games

The tile-based top-down view can be thought of as a grid of images. Every tile in the grid is equal in size, 50 pixels wide by 50 pixels high, and they are arranged in rows and columns. Using this kind of layout is effective because it means a common set of tile images (a *tile set*) can be created and recombined in different grids to make different levels. For example, for Sokoban, one image tile might be the box; another might be some grass, and another could be a pattern of bricks. By simply combining these three different image tiles in a grid, a whole variation of levels can be created that feature walls, floors and boxes. Consider Figure 2.5.

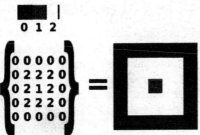

Figure 2.5 The grid and the display

Sokoban will need a specific set of tiles to create its levels. The tiles must include at least the following items. From these, every level of Sokoban can be made.

* **Box** – to be used wherever a box is situated in the level.

* **Grass** – represents a vacant space where either the player can move to, or where a box can be pushed.

* **Brick** – an impassable tile, meaning objects cannot move onto tiles occupied by a brick, and nor can objects move through them.

* **Destination square** – like a grass tile, this is a vacant tile. It appears like an X since it marks the spot where boxes are to be pushed. The player can move into this tile.

* **Player** – the player image must also be a tile, and unlike the other tiles, a player tile will only appear once in any tile grid since there is only one player.

Room for improvement

Further tiles can also be added to this set to increase the diversity of levels and to add all sorts of interesting items. Perhaps in an improved version of Sokoban, power-ups and other diversions can be created.

Designing some grids

Having established a tile set in terms of the images to be used, it becomes possible to design a number of levels for the Sokoban game. If each image in the tile set has a unique number then a grid of numbers can represent a level.

Box = 1, Grass = 2, Brick = 3, Destination square = 4, Player = 5.

The numbers will indicate what each tile in the grid will be. The grid tiles themselves will be referenced like a graph, with the top left tile being (0,0) and the bottom right being (20,20). For this game of Sokoban the grid size has been limited to 20 by 20, though grids could be made larger to accommodate more sizeable levels. Two classic Sokoban levels have been designed and are shown in Figures 2.1 and 2.6. These levels shall feature in our game of Sokoban.

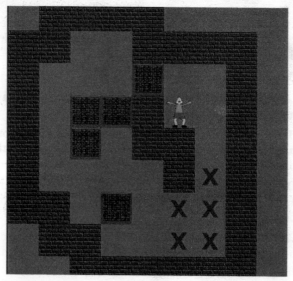

Figure 2.6 A sample level 2 Sokoban layout

- Level 1 is simple and is often the starting level of many Sokoban games. Unlike most levels, it isn't possible for the player to lose this one. There is only one direction the boxes can be pushed and every way leads to a destination square.

- Level 2 is more difficult and many situations lead to a loss. The trouble for many players will be deciding how to push a box onto the destination square in the narrow passageway.

2.4 Tiles and movable objects

In so far as the static level layout is concerned, it's convenient to design the level as one whole grid. That is, for all the items in a level that do not move – walls, floors and destination squares – a single grid is suitable for encoding the level. However, there are two special tile kinds that *can* move or slide, namely the player and any boxes. These can only move within vacant floor tiles so they cannot affect the layout of the level in terms of walls and destination squares. But the player and box positions do affect whether a floor cell is vacant or empty, and this in turn affects whether a box can be pushed. The player cannot step into a square that is occupied by a box. In order to move there the player must push that box in some other direction. Similarly, a box can only be pushed if there's an adjacent square that's empty, i.e. not occupied by a wall or box. So, for each cell that can be occupied by movable objects, there is a status determining whether it is empty or occupied, and this may change as objects are moved.

To suit this purpose, a second grid of the same width and height is added to the design, and it corresponds exactly to the original. The first grid defines the static objects of a level, walls and floors, and the new grid records the positions of movable objects, such as the player and boxes. This works well because a win can be determined by looking for all the destination squares in the original grid and checking to see if there is a box in all the corresponding cells of the movable grid. If there is, a win has occurred. If not, then the game continues.

2.5 Game platform and requirements

When designing a game it's useful to keep in mind the target platform, i.e. the kind of computer the game will work on. This game has been designed for Windows PCs, but it could so easily have been a different system, and at least one version of Sokoban exists for most platforms. This section explores some of today's gaming platforms, though not all of them are freely available to developers. Some, specifically the consoles, require development licences.

PC

PCs are one of the oldest, most diverse and most rapidly changing platforms of them all. Home computers gained popularity largely during the 1970s, after the birth of the microprocessor. Beginning with early, pioneering microcomputers like the Datapoint 2200, ZX Spectrum and Atari ST, the standard IBM PC known today eventually gained prominence. The PC plays an important role for games. It's one of the target platforms for mainstream and independent games alike. Nowadays, the PC can be divided into three sub-platforms reflecting each main operating system.

Windows

Microsoft Windows has the largest market share for any game audience. And, because developers know this, most games for the PC are targeted at least for the Windows operating system. Windows supports a lot of drivers for graphical and sound hardware, making it an easy platform to create fast-paced, exciting games using some of the latest technology.

Mac

The Mac was developed by Apple and first appeared in 1984. It has grown into an established platform for a variety of software. In 1998 the iMac was released and it featured a slick new design and appealing user interface. Since then, Mac has firmly established itself as an exciting alternative games platform with hundreds of titles available.

GNU/Linux

Linux is the ultimate expression of computing freedom, in terms of freedom to change and to distribute software. Linux is often considered to be too complicated for general users, but this is gradually changing with releases like Ubuntu. Many versions of Linux are free, though some are not. And as with the Mac, the number of games available for Linux is increasing. There is also a Wine emulator on Linux, which is software that emulates Windows. This allows Linux users to run many Windows programs.

Playstation (PS1, PS2 and PS3)

The Playstation is a games console created by Sony, who first released PS1 in 1994. Since then, its sequel consoles with new generation technology have been developed, such as the PS2 (2000), and the PS3 (2007). Unlike the PC, the Playstation is a dedicated computer for games, and is not intended to run other software, like spreadsheets or word processors. It's as simple as switching on, putting in a game CD, and then pressing Play. Thankfully, each version of the Playstation is backward compatible with previous versions, which means that games made for previous versions of the computer can run on newer versions; so PS1 games can also run on PS2 and PS3, and PS2 games can also run on PS3. The Playstation is one of the most popular consoles with a large variety of games – made even larger with backward compatibility.

Xbox and Xbox 360

The first Microsoft Xbox was released in 2001, and this was followed at the end of 2005 by the Xbox 360. The Xbox 360 was one of the first to offer an online multiplayer content service. However, there were some complaints regarding the backward compatibility of the Xbox 360, with people reporting that many of their older Xbox games didn't run. Despite this, the Xbox 360 claims to be backward compatible with a large set of Xbox games, with the potential to increase this number as time passes. Due to the large variety of games available, and the current technical abilities of the Xbox, including multiplayer and wireless controllers, it is one of the most popular consoles.

Nintendo consoles

Nintendo is an old name, from the earliest days of home console gaming. As a result, their list of gaming platforms is long, and so is their list of games. Ranging from the NES and Super NES, to later systems such as the Nintendo 64 and Game Cube. Their latest console, the Nintendo Wii (pronounced 'We'), features a unique wireless controller with motion sensitivity in three dimensions, and also sports a number of other features including parental controls, Internet connections and backward compatibility with the Game Cube. Famous games on this platform include the *Mario* and *Zelda* series.

2.6   Sokoban development tools

Having decided that Sokoban will be made for Windows PCs, there are choices to make regarding how to go about developing it. What programming language should be used to make Sokoban? What kinds of game libraries ought to be selected?

Choosing a language: C++

To develop Sokoban, we will use C++. This is a powerful general purpose language used for many games, and favoured by many programmers for its versatility. This book assumes a knowledge of C++ and does not explain the specifics of the language. If you need to know more about it, see *Teach Yourself C++*.

C++ history

C++ has often been called a middle level language because of its combination of high and low level features. The language was developed by a computer scientist called Bjarne Stroustrup in 1983. He based it on an earlier language, C, which was developed by Dennis Ritchie in 1972. Since 1983, C++ has become one of the most prominent languages, and undeniably the most prevalent for games.

For C++ there are two main development programs, also known as IDEs (Integrated Development Environments). These are applications that allow programmers to write and compile software in C++. You only need one of them, and our game could be developed in either one. These IDEs are listed below.

- **Microsoft Visual C++** a popular commercial IDE with a lot of features. The most recent versions include the .NET framework, which is a bundle of classes and functions to make development easier for making Windows software. This IDE can be purchased from many places and is a good choice for general purpose development.

- **Code::Blocks** an exciting and comparatively new IDE. It's free, open source and cross-platform, which means it can run on multiple operating systems, like Windows and Linux. The next chapter explains how to use this IDE. Code::Blocks can be downloaded at: **http://www.codeblocks.org/**.

Libraries

Beyond C++ itself, Sokoban will also make use of a number of libraries. Some of these help draw graphics on the screen and some can play sound and music from common formats like MP3 and OGG. Naturally, for any game there needs to be a way of telling the computer to draw pictures at specific locations on the screen, and there needs to be a way to play music at appropriate times. There are a wide variety of libraries available to game developers for all kinds of purposes. Some are more complete and sophisticated than others; some are free and some expensive. This book considers only libraries that can be downloaded and used for free. Some are free for non-commercial development but require payment if you decide to sell games using them. Sokoban will use a library called SDL for its graphics and BASS Audio for its sound. SDL is free for both commercial and non-commercial use, while BASS Audio is free for non-commercial use only.

Graphics libraries

Graphics libraries offer classes and functions for showing graphics on the screen. They also offer functions to load graphics from files, such as BMP and PNG. In the modern era of gaming, many libraries offer 3D graphics support, hardware acceleration, pixel and vertex shading, and a whole host of other features. The following popular graphics libraries are available.

- **OpenGL (Open Graphics Library)**   one of the industry standard graphics libraries. It's open source, cross-platform and very powerful. It supports hardware-accelerated 2D and 3D graphics, and it is the driving force behind the graphics of some of the most famous games, including the *Myst* series. OpenGL is free for commercial and non-commercial use. More information can be found at: **http://www.opengl.org/**

- **DirectX**   a collection of libraries. Among them, a component called Direct3D is related to both 2D and 3D graphics. Whereas OpenGL is aimed at general-purpose graphics, DirectX tends to be more focused towards games and is for Windows only. It's free but not open source. Like OpenGL, DirectX is a high-powered, high-performance library which supports hardware acceleration. More information can be found at: **http://www.microsoft.com/windows/directx/**

- **SDL (Simple Directmedia Layer)**   this will be used to create the graphics for Sokoban. SDL is a quick, simple-to-use library aimed at creating graphics for games. It has a long history, is widely documented, is free for both commercial and non-commercial use, and is cross-platform. SDL can work on an impressive list of different operating systems, including: Linux, Windows, Windows CE, BeOS, MacOS, Mac OS X, FreeBSD, NetBSD, OpenBSD, BSD/OS, Solaris, IRIX, and QNX. It also can be used on: AmigaOS, Dreamcast, Atari, AIX, OSF/Tru64, RISC OS, SymbianOS, and OS/2. SDL is covered in a later chapter, but more information can be found at: **http://www.libsdl.org/**

Sound libraries

Sound libraries offer functions and classes for playing sound and music. Sound can come in many kinds of formats and files, like MP3, OGG, and WAV, to name some of them. Some specific formats are discussed in Chapter 5. For now, some of the available sound libraries can be summarized as follows.

- **OpenAL (Open Audio Library)**   often seen as a counterpart to OpenGL. It's free for commercial and non-commercial use, is cross-platform and is open source. It can play sound in various formats and can achieve some impressive surround sound effects, and 3D sound. More information can be found at: **http://www.openal.org/**

- **FMOD** this audio library is a popular industry choice, because it's simple to use and very powerful. It is free for non-commercial only, and though it is not open source it supports a wide range of current gaming platforms. These include: Win32, Win64, WinCE, Linux, Linux64, Macintosh (os8/9/10/x86) PS2, PSP, PS3, Xbox, Xbox 360, Game Cube, and Wii. FMOD supports a long list of audio formats. More information can be found at: http://www.fmod.org/

- **BASS** this library will be used for programming the sound for Sokoban. It is an ideal choice as it's simple to use and very powerful. It supports a long list of popular audio formats and is cross-platform. It is free only for non-commercial use, but reduced prices are available for small independent game makers intending to use BASS for commercial products. BASS is explained in more detail later, but more information can be found at: http://www.un4seen.com/

Summary

In this chapter the general case for creating Sokoban has been made. The rules of the game have been defined and two levels have been established. These levels will include a variety of tiles from a tile set. This set includes walls, floors, destination squares, boxes and the player. Naturally, more levels could be added and more tile types could also be added to enrich the experience. The language of C++ has been chosen to create the game and the SDL and Bass Audio libraries have been selected to create the graphics and sound.

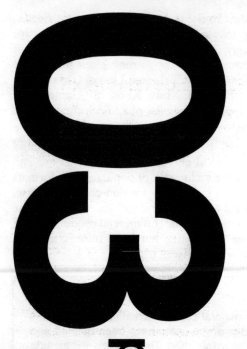

03 programming

In this chapter you will learn about:

- C++
- Visual C++ and Code::Blocks
- STL
- strings and lists
- game loops

Tell me where is fancy bred, Or in the heart or in the head?
William Shakespeare (*The Merchant of Venice*)

3.1 C++ integrated development

To program in C++, you need a development environment. This is an application which lets you write and compile C++ programs. Some readers might already have a development environment with which they are familiar, and others might be interested in seeing some options.

Microsoft Visual C++ (VC++)

Microsoft Visual C++ is a commercial IDE and can be purchased from a number of retailers, both on the high street and online. It is now part of the Microsoft Visual Studio .NET suite of applications, and the latest version (at the time of writing) is 2005. It is a popular choice among developers generally, because it is simple to use, and many third party libraries are compatible with

Figure 3.1 The Visual C++ screen

its compiler, so that lots of libraries just plug-in and go. Visual Studio is packaged with the .NET runtime library, but this book will not make use of the .NET framework itself. Instead, its focus will be on C++, and on the SDL and BASS libraries since these are designed with games in mind and are cross-platform.

Introducing Microsoft Visual C++

Visual C++ is usually installed from a CD or DVD as part of the Visual Studio installation. It will appear as a selectable option from the Start menu. The Visual Studio interface offers a lot of different options for creating C++ applications. Figure 3.2 shows the **File > New > Project** menu.

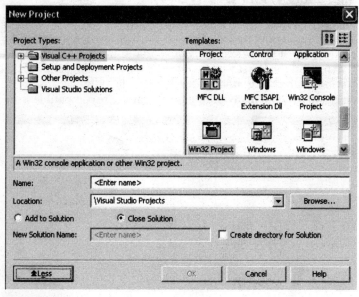

Figure 3.2 Starting a new project

For games, a blank Win32 project is a good place to start; a basic .NET Forms application is also suitable. Games rely on third-party libraries and make little use of the Windows API. For this reason the best project to start from is the one which makes as little use of memory as possible.

To create a blank Win32 project in Visual C++:

1 Click **File > New > Project**.

2 Select *Win 32 Project* from the Template list.

3 Enter a project **Name** and **Location**. This will be where the project is saved and loaded from the hard disk.

4 Click **OK**.

5 In **Application Settings**, select *Empty Project*.

6 Click **Finish** to create the project.

Creating and adding files to a project

A project is the collective name for a group of C++ source and header files. When executed, these together make up the program. To one edge of the screen in Visual C++, is the **Solution Explorer** which displays all the files that are currently part of the active project. For a blank project, this pane will list no files. Instead the list will simply have a number of folder categories; Source Files, Header Files and Resource Files.

To add a new source or header file to the project:

1 Click **Project > Add New Item...**

2 From the template list select a file to add, often this will be a source file (.cpp) or a header file (.h).

3 Enter a name and location.

4 Click **OK**.

To add an existing source or header file to the project:

1 Click **Project > Add Existing Item...**

2 Select the file from the **Open File** dialog box.

Setting project properties

When developing games, especially when using external libraries, it is important to make sure header files and lib files are situated in appropriate directories. Projects will need to include header files and link to libraries. Therefore, it's essential to make their path information available to the compiler, otherwise it cannot find where header files are and it cannot link to libraries. In this book, a number of libraries will be used and their path information must be specified in the Project Properties.

To add a header file directory to the search list:

1• Click **Project > Properties**.

2• In the list view, select **C/C++ > General**.

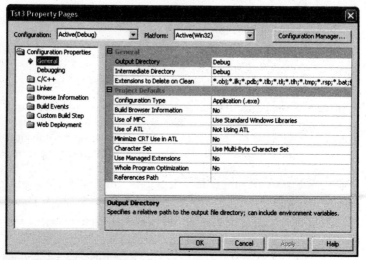

Figure 3.3 Setting properties

3• Add a path to the **Additional Include Directories** edit box (e.g. c:\source\inc\).

To add a library file directory to the search list:

1   Click **Project > Properties**.

2   In the list view, select **Linker > General**.

3   Add a path to the **Additional Library Directories** edit box.

To add a library (lib) file to link:

1   Click **Project > Properties**.

2   In the list view, select **Linker > Input**.

3   Add a library file to the **Additional Dependencies** edit box (e.g. BASS.lib).

Code::Blocks

Code::Blocks is an exciting and comparatively new alternative to Microsoft Visual C++. It's free, open source, cross-platform and easy to use. Unlike Visual C++, it doesn't come with the

.NET framework, but is a more lightweight development environment. Code::Blocks is ideal for developing games, because it works with the majority of game libraries, including SDL, DirectX and OpenGL. Furthermore, Code::Blocks includes a number of project templates and wizards to set up and configure game development projects for you.

Supported compilers for Code::Blocks

- GCC (MingW / Linux GCC)
- Microsoft Visual C++
- Digital Mars
- Borland C++ 5.5
- Open Watcom

Downloading Code::Blocks

The Code::Blocks website is **http://www.codeblocks.org/**. There are two versions that can be downloaded:

- The main stable release is the one the developers make available for wide distribution since it is the most reliable.
- The developmental version is the one the developers are currently working on. This might contain more bugs, but it will include the latest features.

Creating new projects with Code::Blocks

Code::Blocks features a number of project templates from which new projects can be created. Like in Visual C++, Code::Blocks projects will organize together all the source and header files that make up a C++ program.

To create a new project, click **File > New > Project**. This will display the New Project dialog box. Code::Blocks has been designed with game developers in mind and there are many easy-to-use project wizards and templates (see Figure 3.5). A suitable start might be a blank project or a simple Win32 project. In the next chapter, the SDL project wizard will be used to create a new SDL project for programming the graphics for Sokoban.

- Code::Blocks can import and convert a number of existing projects from other IDEs, such as Visual C++ and Dev C++. To do this, click **File > Import**.

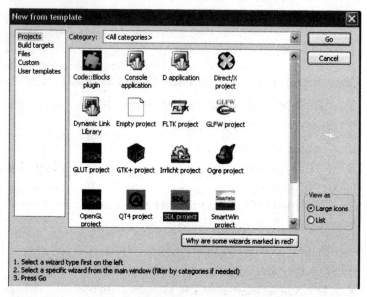

Figure 3.4 The Code::Blocks interface

Figure 3.5 Starting from a project wizard or template in Code::Blocks

Creating and adding files to a project

A new project may either be blank (contain no files), or it may contain some source and header files, depending on its type. New files, and existing files, can be added to a project. The left-hand pane on the screen is called the *Project Workspace Tree*, and it shows all the files in the current project.

To add a new source or header file to the project:

1 Click **File > New > File**.

2 From the list, select the type of file to add, source or header. Click **Go**.

3 The **Add New File** wizard begins. Click **Next**.

4 Enter the path and name of the file to add. Click **OK**.

To add an existing source or header file to the project:

1 Click **Project > Add Files**.

2 Select the file(s) to add from the **Open File** dialog box.

Setting project properties

Code::Blocks provides a number of project wizards, and these configure compiler build options automatically for you. However, it's useful to know how header files, source files and other directories can be added to the compiler search path manually. This section also explains how specific lib files can be linked to.

To add a header file directory to the search list:

1 Click **Project > Build Options**.

2 Click the **Directories** tab.

3 On the **Compiler** tab, click **Add** to select a folder (e.g. c:\source\inc\).

To add a library file directory to the search list:

1 Click **Project > Build Options**.

2 Click the **Directories** tab.

3 Click the **Linker** tab.

4 Click **Add** to select a folder (e.g. c:\source\lib\).

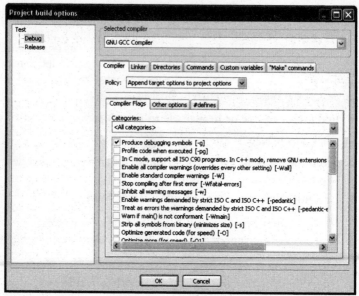

Figure 3.6 The Project Build options dialogue box

To add a library (lib) file to link to:

1 Click **Project > Build Options**.

2 Select the **Linker** tab.

3 Click **Add** to select a library file (e.g. BASS.lib).

3.2 Debugging with Visual C++ and Code::Blocks

To run a C++ program, it must be compiled.

To compile a program:

* In Visual C++, click **Build > Compile**, or press [Ctrl] + [F7].

* In Code::Blocks, click the blue cog icon or press [Ctrl]+ [F9].

To run a program:

* In Visual C++, click the **Play** button on the toolbar, or press [F5] on the keyboard.

* In Code::Blocks, press [F8].

In combination with running a program, both IDEs offer a wide range of debugging facilities to help locate and track runtime errors in your software. Here are some of the more useful.

Debug

Press [F5] in VC++ or [F8] in Code::Blocks to run Debug in normal mode. The program will run normally unless interrupted by an error or a *breakpoint*. If an error occurs during runtime, the debugging will highlight and display the line of code where the error occurred. A breakpoint can be set to mark a place in the source files where the program is to pause for debugging. This is so the state of variables can be examined, and programmers can also use this in combination with *Stepping* to watch the flow of execution, line by line. To examine the contents of a variable during debugging, you can drag and drop the variables into the Watches pane, which appears when debugging is active.

Breakpoints

Breakpoints are like bookmarks in source code. They mark places where execution should pause during debugging. A source file can contain more than one breakpoint.

- **Visual C++**. To set a breakpoint, click the right-hand mouse button on the line where it is to be set. A context menu appears – select **Insert Breakpoint**. Removing a breakpoint is similar to adding. Click the right-hand button on a line containing a breakpoint, and select **Remove Breakpoint**.

- **Code::Blocks**. To set a breakpoint, click the right-hand mouse button on the line where a breakpoint needs to be set. A context menu appears – select **Toggle Breakpoint**. Removing a breakpoint is the same as adding.

Stepping

When an error is encountered or a breakpoint is hit, it's useful to continue execution while watching over how it flows and steps through the source code. Stepping comes in two forms:

- Step Into ([F11] in VC++) or ([Shift]+[F7] in Code::Blocks).
- Step Over ([F10] in VC++) or ([F7] in Code::Blocks).

These operations are responsible for stepping through the code, line by line. If a function call is encountered during stepping, the Step Into command will enter the function where you can step through this too. Step Over will run the function without entering it and debugging will resume at the next line of code.

3.3 Getting started with STL

From this point on, this book will remain IDE independent and not make assumptions about which one you may have chosen. We will start to explore programming in preparation for making Sokoban. The first subject to consider is the STL (**Standard Template Library**) which may be familiar to some readers. The STL is a library of general-purpose functions and classes for managing memory, sorting data in arrays, representing strings, and so on. Though our game will not draw too heavily upon the STL library, there are a number of classes on offer that are especially useful to games generally. Specifically, these classes are:

- **std::string**. A dynamic string class. Instead of using limited and finite char arrays, std::string can store variable length strings and offers a range of methods to make string manipulation easier. This class will be used to store filenames and other kinds of string data.

- **std::vector**. This is a linked list template class. It can be used to store a variable length list of all kinds of data. For example, in a game where the player wanders around and collects different items, the std::vector class can be used to keep track of all the items collected in one long array. Later sections in this chapter examine std::vector.

NOTE. To include these classes in your C++ projects, the headers <string> and <vector> must be included. Example:

```
#include <string>
#include <vector>
```

> STL and SDL are different libraries: STL (Standard Template Library) and SDL (Simple Directmedia Layer). Both are considered in this book. STL does not need to be downloaded separately, as it ships with both the C++ IDEs mentioned in this book.

3.4 Using std::string

When people first learn C++, they are shown how to code strings by using a char array, such as char MyString[50];. The problem with this method is that, in the example, the string cannot be more than 50 characters long. So if the player entered a name longer than this, the string would be truncated. Similarly, if the player entered a name that was less, then memory would be wasted on storing extra characters. The problem would be even worse if advanced string handling was needed, such as inserting characters at specific positions. How could you insert the letter 'e' in the middle of a string? Or how could you add two strings together, like "hello" and "world"?

The std::string class attempts to solve such problems. Using this class, strings can be assigned to string variables just as integers can be assigned to integer variables, using the = equality operator. Furthermore, std::strings can be added together, characters can be inserted and deleted, and the string is dynamic. That is, it will grow or shrink in memory to accommodate all the characters. So, new characters can be added and removed at runtime, and the string will always be large enough to hold them.

Creating and combining a std::string object

To create a std::string object consider the following code. Note how a string can be assigned to the object cleanly and simply.

```
std::string MyString1 = "Hello";
std::string MyString2 = "world";

// MyString3 = "helloworld"
std::string MyString3 = MyString1 + MyString2;
```

The length of a std::string

The length of a string refers to how many characters it contains. It can be zero or more. To return the length of a std::string object, the **length** method can be used.

```
std::string MyString1 = "Hello World";

//string_length = 11
int string_length = MyString1.length();
```

Inserting, replacing and erasing

The std::string class also has methods to insert characters into a string, replace existing characters and to erase characters. Consider the sample code.

Inserting

```
string str1 = "abcdefghi";
string str2 = "0123";
str1.insert (3,str2); // "abc0123defghi"
```

Replacing

```
string str1 = "abcdefghi";
string str2 = "XYZ";
str1.replace (4,2,str2); // "abcdXYZghi"
```

Erasing

```
std::string str = "abcdefghi";
str.erase (5,3); // "abcdei"
```

Converting

Though it's convenient to deal with std::strings, there are many libraries that expect the older null-terminated string arguments such as type char*, but std::string is not compatible with this type. However, std:string does feature a c_str method. This function returns a converted char* string based on a std::string.

```
std::string str = "abcdefghi";
const char* converted_string = str.c_str();
```

Substrings

std::string can also return a substring of a specified length. A substring is a smaller string of the std::string object. It begins at a specified index (position in the string) and is a specified number of characters long.

```
string str1 = "abcdefghi"
string str2 = str1.substr (6,2); // "gh"
```

3.5   Using std::vector

The STL std::vector class works like a C++ array in that it can store a set of zero or more objects of the same type. It also lets you use the standard subscript operator to access each element in the array, such as MyList[5]. However, it has some important differences to the standard array. First, it is a *template class*, which means it can be customized to hold objects of any type – int, float, std::string, and so on. Next, it is a dynamic list. This means it is not a fixed size like an ordinary array, but grows and shrinks so it has enough room to hold as many objects as needed. And finally, it contains a number of methods to return the size of the list, the first and the last items, and other functions.

Creating a list and adding an item

To create a vector of integers and a vector of std::strings, consider the following code. Notice how the object type is specified in the angle brackets (<>).

```
std::vector<int> List_Of_Numbers;
std::vector<std::string> List_Of_Strings;

//Add an item to each one
int Number = 1;
std::string Str = "hello world";

List_Of_Numbers.push_back(Number);
List_Of_Strings.push_back(Str);
```

Cycling through items

Each element in the list can be accessed using the ([]) subscript operator. Furthermore, the **size** method of std::vector can return the number of items being held in the list. This can be used to cycle through all items in the list.

```
for (unsigned int indx = 0; indx <
  vec_list.size(); indx++)
{
  //Access to each item
  int Number = vec_list[indx];
}
```

3.6 The game loop

The previous sections examined some of the fundamental classes of the STL, std::string and std::vector. These classes will be used by Sokoban to handle strings and to store lists of data, as will be shown later. The last subject to consider in this chapter in preparation for Sokoban is the game loop. This is not part of the STL nor is it a class. It is a programming construct that is useful for all games. It requires us to think a little differently from how we understand other software to work.

Non-game software

Most applications are designed to respond to user input and they don't usually function while the user isn't operating them. For example, a word processor or spreadsheet will format the text, check spelling and check punctuation as the user presses keys on the keyboard. Similarly, if the user wants to print a document they press the Print button. All of these operations require user input. It is based on event-driven programming. If the user tells the software to do something, then it does it. If there is no input from the user then it does nothing.

Games

However, when we think about games in this way, we will see that they do not work like a word processor or spreadsheet. For example, imagine a first-person shooting game where a number of contestants must shoot each other in an arena. There are the player and the enemies. Even if the player doesn't press a single key on the keyboard, even if the player never moves a muscle, the enemies still run around and take part. The game still runs smoothly, consistently and independently of whether the user takes part. In fact, even when the player sits there doing nothing, the game could still be chugging along at several hundred frames per second. For this reason, the basic architecture of a game needs to work differently from standard software.

Creating the game loop

Standard Windows applications work by event-driven programming. Applications receive notifications from the Windows operating system about events that happen on the system. These events might be a key press, a mouse click and so on. The notifications arrive to applications in the form of messages. As they arrive, such as an instruction to print a document, applications process them, then wait for more. This process repeats until the application ends. Games, however, need to take more control.

Think about it like this: as a game begins it enters a standard C++ **while** loop, and continues looping until the player hits the Exit button or presses the Escape key. This loop is common among games and is known as the *game loop*. Each iteration of the loop is called a *frame*, and on each frame, the game must check and handle several important tasks. It should check for input from the player, update its graphics, update its sound and all the other variables that might change over time. The following pseudo code shows a basic game loop.

```
while(user doesn't exit)
   check for user input
   draw graphics
   play sounds
   do AI & move enemies
end while
```

On each frame a game should:

- **Update input.** Rather than wait on messages and notifications about user input, the game polls the keyboard and mouse on each frame. It does this to determine whether it needs to respond. For example, it checks to see, among other things, the position of the mouse cursor and which keys on the keyboard are pressed.

- **Update graphics.** In standard applications, Windows automatically handles the drawing of buttons, edit boxes and all the other controls a user might find in a window. However, a game is responsible for drawing its own graphics to the game window, and it needs to do this on each frame. This includes game characters, effects, 3D objects and so on. For Sokoban, this means drawing the level; the boxes, the player, the destination squares and so on.

- **Update sound.** Some games need to update their sound on each frame too. Here, most games check to see if specific sounds must stop playing, and whether other ones need to start playing. For example, if an enemy stops firing their gun, the game must stop the gunshot sounds from playing.

• **Update physics and AI.** If the game is intelligent it also needs to respond. For example, enemy soldiers do not stand still doing nothing. They typically move about independently of the player, and they do so in an intelligent way. Furthermore, the game might include physical reactions, perhaps something simple like a character moving from one place to another. In this case, the game must update the position of objects and characters, according to their speed and so on.

Sample game loop

This section demonstrates a real C++ game loop at work. This is not a game loop for the Sokoban game; but it is an overall demonstration of game loops generally. Later chapters will illustrate the game loop more clearly in the context of Sokoban. Consider the following code.

```
bool done = false;
 while (!done) //Loop until quit
 {
 HandleMessages();
 //Process any important windows messages

 Update();
 //Update game. Draw graphics, update input...
}
```

Summary

This chapter introduced two different IDEs suited to games development in C++, Visual C++ and Code::Blocks. It also explored the Standard Template Library and introduced the std::string and std::vector classes. These classes will prove valuable for the tasks ahead in creating Sokoban. std::string will be used to handle strings throughout the code in this book, and std::vector will be used to manage lists of objects. Finally, the game loop was considered in some detail.

04

graphics programming

In this chapter you will learn:

- about graphics libraries
- about SDL
- how to draw graphics
- about surfaces and blitting
- about colour keying
- about page flipping

Program testing can be used to show the presence of bugs, but never to show their absence.

Edsger Dijkstra

4.1 Graphics

Our game is to include two levels and the objective of each is to push a set of boxes onto a number of destination squares. The purpose of this chapter is to show how game graphics are programmed, and the SDL library will be used to achieve this. Though the ideas presented here are considered in the context of Sokoban, they could as easily be applied to any game the reader may choose. A computer game's graphics are its visual images. Some graphics are 3D, some 2D and others can be a mixed variety. For the purposes of Sokoban and this book, the graphics are a 2D kind.

2D graphics

Cartoons, hand-drawn sketches, paintings and photos are all examples of 2D graphics. They cannot be viewed from other angles, and they cannot be rotated to see the other side. Tile-based games like Sokoban use 2D graphics.

3D graphics

3D graphics are like sculptures and can be seen from all kinds of angles since they're objects occupying 3D space. There are, in computing terms, two kinds of 3D graphics; pre-rendered 3D and realtime 3D. In modern games, realtime 3D is the most common. These update and change as events unfold in the game. They are found in most modern first-person shooters like *Quake* and *Doom*. Pre-rendered are 3D graphics created beforehand and stored for later display. These are made in 3D software and include the kind featured in films.

NOTE. Graphics have been created on computers ever since the creation of Sketchpad in 1962 and are now commonplace in films. This was not always the case. In 1979 a film called *The Works* was planned to be the world's first feature-length movie made entirely from computer animation. This film was never completed and in 1995 Pixar's *Toy Story* would claim that record.

4.2 Creating graphics

Before looking at graphics programming it's worth examining briefly how game graphics are created. The graphics for Sokoban are a set of tileable images 50 pixels wide by 50 pixels high. They were created in a standard Photo Program, called GIMP. These sorts of images can be made by hand or by mouse, or they can be obtained from third parties. Some places provide images for a fee, and others provide them freely via the Creative Common Licence so long as you do not intend using them for commercial purposes. The majority of games on the market today feature 3D graphics designed by in-house artists using sophisticated software. This section explores some of the facilities and software available for making game graphics.

Graphics hardware

Scanners

Scanners transfer images onto a computer. There are two main types of scanner, hand-held and flat bed. Flat beds are now the most common. They work like photocopiers and can transfer your sketches, paintings and photos to the computer. Scanners have now become affordable devices for the home and offer an easy way of importing 2D graphics.

Graphics tablets

Less widely known than scanners, are graphics tablets. These work like an electronic paper and pen. Artists can draw freehand onto a touch-sensitive surface. The device then feeds this information into the computer and generates a corresponding picture.

Graphics software

Photoshop and GIMP

These two applications are a form of photo-editing software. They can accept pictures from scanners and graphics tablets and also provide tools for making images using the mouse. Additionally they can save and edit common image files, like BMP, JPEG, PNG and so on. Photoshop is a commercial application. GIMP can be downloaded for free from **http://www.gimp.org/**.

3DS Max and Blender 3D

For creating 3D graphics there are 3DS Max and Blender 3D. These programs let artists create models, like a sculpture made from clay. Artists model worlds and characters using a set of tools. The software also offers texturing features so artists can colour their models and wallpaper them with realistic-looking images. 3DS Max is a commercial application.

Blender 3D is free, and can be downloaded from **http://www.blender.org/**.

4.3 Graphics and SDL

Game graphics can be created in various ways, as previous sections have shown. The graphics for Sokoban consist of 2D tiles only, equal in width and height. The images will be stored in standard bitmap files. So our game needs a way of loading the images into memory and then drawing them to the screen at specified positions. This is one of the main intentions of any graphics library, and for Sokoban the SDL library will be used. SDL is an acronym for *Simple Directmedia Layer*. It's free, open source and cross-platform. In short, SDL is a fun and powerful way to draw game graphics.

> This book considers SDL using C++. However, SDL is compliant with other languages too. These include: C, Ada, C#, Eiffel, Erlang, Euphoria, Guile, Haskell, Java, Lisp, Lua, ML, Objective C, Pascal, Perl, PHP, Pike, Pliant, Python, Ruby, and Smalltalk.

4.4 Downloading and installing SDL

To get started, the SDL library must be downloaded from **http://www.libsdl.org/**. The current version at the time of writing is 1.2, and the site includes all the development files necessary to build SDL 1.2 applications; files such as source, header and lib files. The website also includes a number of other important packages, including runtime libraries and documentation. These are the packages available for download.

SDL GPG Signed Source Code

This is the actual SDL source code for the entire library. Though informative, and essential if you plan to make changes to the library, this package is not required for making games with the SDL. This book doesn't recommend downloading this package.

SDL runtime libraries

For Windows, this package includes the file *SDL.dll*. It is not required for developing SDL applications, but it is for running them on a system. The DLL file needs to be in the same directory as the game EXE before it is run, or in the *Windows/System* directory. The runtime package is an essential download, and any users of your game will also need it. Chapter 9 shows how games can be distributed by creating installation packages.

Development libraries

These are the main sets of files for developers and contain all the headers and lib files required for compiling SDL programs. They are essential. There are two packages to choose from.

For Visual C++:

SDL-devel-1.2.11-VC6.zip

For Code::Blocks:

SDL-devel-1.2.11-mingw32.tar.gz

This latter package is not required for running SDL games, and so users of your game will not need these files.

Documentation

This is an optional package, but is recommended. It includes all the HTML and Help files for SDL as a reference. It lists all the classes of SDL, all the functions and arguments, and is a general knowledge base for SDL developers. It most certainly doesn't need to be distributed to users of your game.

Configuring SDL for Visual C++

For Visual C++ the **SDL-devel-1.2.11-VC6.zip** developmental package should have been downloaded and extracted to a location on the local computer.

To configure the package for use in Visual C++:

1 Start a new *Empty Win32 Project*.

2 From the SDL directory, either copy all the *lib* and *include* directories into the VC++ existing *lib* and *include* directories. Or, select **Project > Properties** and configure the *include* and *linker* paths to the appropriate SDL folders, as discussed in the previous chapter, *Setting project properties* (page 31).

3 Two library files must be linked. These can be specified in **Project > Properties**, under the **Additional Dependencies** section (See Chapter 3). These files are: *sdl.lib* and *sdlmain.lib*.

4 In **Project > Properties > C/C++ Code Generation**, set **Runtime Library** to *Multi-Threaded DLL (/MD)*.

5 Add a new source file to the project (see page 31). Insert this code and compile:

```
#include <SDL.h>

int main(int argc, char* args[])
{
  return 0;
}
```

Configuring SDL for Code::Blocks

For Code::Blocks the **SDL-devel-1.2.11-mingw32.tar.gz** package should have been downloaded and extracted onto the local computer. Configuring this for use in Code::Blocks is really easy.

To set up Code::Blocks to compile SDL applications:

1 Click **File > New > Project**.

2 Select *SDL Project* and click **OK**.

3 You may be asked to specify the SDL path. In this case, select the directory where SDL was installed. This directory should contain *include* and *lib* subdirectories.

4 Enter the project name and path. Click **Finish**. The application is ready to compile and run.

The Code::Blocks SDL wizard will already have created a sample SDL application. This will include a series of SDL function calls and examples.

4.5   Getting started with SDL

Generally, SDL is used to program game graphics, but it can
also perform a number of other tasks. SDL can play audio and
music, it can control access to the CD-ROM (ejecting, etc.), and
can read input from gaming devices like joysticks. Each of these
components SDL calls a *subsystem*. Naturally, the main subsystem is that for drawing graphics, which is the video subsystem –
not video in the sense of movies or mpg files, but in the sense of
graphics cards. The rest of this chapter examines the video component with an aim to drawing graphics for Sokoban.

> You do not need to create an application window. Often .NET
> is used to do this, but SDL creates windows for you.

Initializing SDL

The first function any SDL application must call is **SDL_Init**.
This will probably be the first thing inside the main function. It
is an initialization function that prepares the SDL library for
further work. SDL will not operate correctly unless it has been
called. It accepts one integer argument *flags*, and returns -1 or 0,
where -1 means an error occurred and 0 means the function
succeeded. If the function succeeded, then SDL is ready to go.

```
int SDL_Init(Uint32 flags);
```

Argument list

flags – specifies which subsystem to initialize. For Sokoban this
will be SDL_INIT_VIDEO. It can also be any of the following:

```
SDL_INIT_TIMER
SDL_INIT_AUDIO
SDL_INIT_CDROM
SDL_INIT_JOYSTICK
SDL_INIT_EVERYTHING
```

Sample code

```
if ( SDL_Init( SDL_INIT_VIDEO ) < 0 )
{
  printf( "Unable to init SDL: %s\n",
  SDL_GetError() );
}
```

SDL_GetError() returns a string describing the last SDL error to occur, if any. This makes it a good function to print to files or to the screen if, and when, errors occur.

Creating a window and setting the video mode

The previous section initialized SDL, but this did not create a window or change the resolution. If the program were run right now, then nothing would appear; the program would begin and then end right away. So more work needs to be done. Next, the game window.

Sokoban will not change the resolution, but it will run in a window. Some games opt to change the resolution and run in full screen to create an immersible experience, but this approach is not appropriate for Sokoban. The **SDL_SetVideoMode** function is used to achieve these kinds of ends. It creates a game window of a width and height specified in pixels, and the *flags* argument can be set to a range of values, which can set the game to full screen or window mode, and can change resolution.

```
SDL_Surface *SDL_SetVideoMode(int width, int
  height, int bpp, Uint32 flags);
```

Argument list

width – width of window in pixels.

height – height of window in pixels.

bbp – bits per pixel. This can be 16.

flags – can be a combination of values telling SDL how to create a window and set up the display. For a complete list, please consult the documentation. Some of the most useful are:

- SDL_SWSURFACE – sets SDL to perform graphics processing in system memory, giving slower performance but wider compatibility between systems.

- SDL_HWSURFACE – sets SDL to perform graphics processing on the graphics card, producing faster performance but placing greater demand on graphics hardware. Sokoban will use this option.

- SDL_FULLSCREEN – if this flag is included, it will set the application to full screen mode.

Sample code

```
SDL_Surface *screen = SDL_SetVideoMode(800, 600,
  16,SDL_HWSURFACE|SDL_DOUBLEBUF);
```

SDL_SetVideoMode returns an **SDL_Surface** pointer (see page 56).

4.6 SDL game loop

In the last section, an SDL application was initialized and a window was created, but if the application as it stands were to be compiled and run it wouldn't last long – a window might flicker on the screen and then vanish. This is because there isn't a game loop running to sustain the life of the application. It enters the main function then drops out. A game loop continues looping until it is told to exit by the user. Upon exiting, the loop – and therefore, the game – will end. The exit condition will usually be when the user presses [Esc] or clicks the Quit button. A sample game loop for an SDL application might appear as follows.

```
// initialize SDL video
  if ( SDL_Init( SDL_INIT_VIDEO ) < 0 )
  {
    printf( "Unable to init SDL: %s\n",
      SDL_GetError() );
    return 1;
  }

  // create a new window
  SDL_Surface *screen = SDL_SetVideoMode(800,
    600, 16, SDL_HWSURFACE|SDL_DOUBLEBUF);
  if ( !screen )
  {
    printf("Unable to set 800x600 video: %s\n",
  SDL_GetError());
    return 1;
  }
  //Enter Game Loop

  bool done = false;
  while (!done)
```

```
{
  // message processing loop
  SDL_Event event;
  while (SDL_PollEvent(&event))
  {
    // check for messages
    switch (event.type)
    {
      // exit if the window is closed
      case SDL_QUIT:
        done = true;
        break;
      // check for keypresses
      case SDL_KEYDOWN:
      {
        //Handle key presses
        break;
      }
    } // end switch
  } // end of message processing
  //Do game update
  //Update Graphics
  //Update Input
}
//Do exit
```

SDL event processing

The sample code demonstrates an SDL game loop. On each frame
it updates game graphics and input, etc., and it also polls SDL
for any events. Events can be exit commands, key presses, mouse
movements, and so on. Here, the example asks SDL about the
state of the keyboard, whether the user is pressing any key and it
also checks to see whether the user pressed [Esc]. Naturally, pressing this will break from the loop. Events can be polled sequentially
in SDL using the **SDL_PollEvent** function. This accepts a pointer
to an **SDL_Event** structure, which will receive information about
an event. Only one event is returned per call to **SDL_PollEvent**.
So since many events can happen, sometimes simultaneously,
the events get queued, meaning an application should loop until
there are no more events to poll. **SDL_PollEvent** returns NULL
when there are no more events on the queue.

Event structure

```
typedef union{
  Uint8 type;
  SDL_ActiveEvent active;
  SDL_KeyboardEvent key;
  SDL_MouseMotionEvent motion;
  SDL_MouseButtonEvent button;
  SDL_JoyAxisEvent jaxis;
  SDL_JoyBallEvent jball;
  SDL_JoyHatEvent jhat;
  SDL_JoyButtonEvent jbutton;
  SDL_ResizeEvent resize;
  SDL_ExposeEvent expose;
  SDL_QuitEvent quit;
  SDL_UserEvent user;
  SDL_SywWMEvent syswm;
} SDL_Event;
```

Each **SDL_Event** structure polled from function **SDL_PollEvent** describes a unique event. In SDL there are a number of established event types: key press, mouse click, etc. You can check the event type by examining the type member of SDL_Event. For a complete list please consult the SDL documentation, but these are the most common:

SDL_QUIT

One of the most important events in an SDL application. This event is returned when the user decides to quit, e.g. when they click the Close button of the window. At this stage an application should end the loop and perform any clean up operations.

SDL_KEYDOWN

This event occurs when the user presses a key on the keyboard. Once received, the actual SDL key code of the key pressed is stored in the **keysym** member of SDL_Event.

SDL_MOUSEBUTTONDOWN

This event is triggered when a mouse button is pressed. When received, the x and y coordinates of the cursor (relative to the top left corner of the screen) are stored in x and y members of SDL_Event. The button numbers of {SDL_BUTTON_LEFT,

SDL_BUTTON_MIDDLE, SDL_BUTTON_RIGHT} are stored in the button member of SDL_MouseButtonEvent.

Running the application at this point will work. A window will appear on screen and remain there until the user decides to exit. However, the window will be blank. Now it's time to examine how graphics are loaded and drawn.

4.7 SDL surfaces

The process of drawing images to the screen involves *surfaces*. The main surface was created in the call to **SDL_SetVideoMode**. It was returned as a **SDL_Surface** pointer. A surface in general represents a rectangle of contiguous bytes in memory. Sometimes it will be in system memory, and other times it will be in video hardware memory; this depends on the creation flags used for SDL_SetVideoMode. Surfaces hold image data. Images can be loaded from standard files like JPG and BMP; they can also be copied to and from other surfaces and they can be drawn onto like canvases. So several smaller surfaces loaded from image files can be combined on a larger surface. The surface created with SDL_SetVideoMode represents the window, so any surface copied to this during the game loop will be drawing its contents to the window.

Creating surfaces from files

Surfaces can be loaded from files using the **SDL_LoadBMP** function. It accepts a valid file path as an argument and returns an **SDL_Surface** pointer. If the function failed, this pointer will be NULL; otherwise, this will be a pointer to a valid image surface in memory.

```
SDL_Surface *SDL_LoadBMP(const char *file);
```

Argument list

file – path to a valid image file. Though this argument is type char*, std::string types can be converted to char* (see page 40).

Sample code

```
SDL_Surface*Surface=SDL_LoadBMP(Filename.c_str());
```

Remember to delete the surface when it's no longer needed, using the **SDL_FreeSurface** function. For each successful call to SDL_LoadBMP there should be a corresponding call to SDL_FreeSurface. This function accepts as its argument a pointer to a surface to be deleted.

Optimizing surfaces

When SDL_SetVideoMode is called to create a game window, it is possible to specify the colour depth of the window in terms of bits per pixel – 16, 24 or 32, etc. This defines the range of possible colours an image can display. The higher this number, the more colours that can be shown; but more colours also require more memory and more processing power. For the Sokoban game, 16 bits per pixel (bpp) was specified. This gives us 65,536 colours to use.

Individual image files also have their own formats of bits per pixel, and these may differ from that of the game window. This means when two surfaces of different formats are copied onto one another, the source surface must be converted to the destination format. Otherwise, the surfaces will not display correctly. Since an SDL application copies surfaces to the window on each frame, it will incur a performance penalty if a conversion needs to happen every time. For this reason, SDL has the function **SDL_DisplayFormat** to convert surfaces to the window format beforehand. It's a one-off conversion and well worth doing. The function accepts a pointer to a surface and returns a new surface. Typically, programmers call **SDL_DisplayFormat** immediately after loading a surface using **SDL_LoadBMP**.

```
SDL_Surface *SDL_DisplayFormat(SDL_Surface
  *surface);
```

Argument list

surface – pointer to a valid surface that is to be converted to the window colour depth.

Sample code

```
SDL_Surface *Tmp = SDL_LoadBMP(Filename.c_str());
  SDL_Surface* bmp = NULL;
```

```
if(Tmp)
{
   bmp = SDL_DisplayFormat(Tmp);
   SDL_FreeSurface(Tmp);
}
```

Copying surfaces

The term *blitting* is used to describe copying among surfaces. Surfaces can be copied completely or partially; a rectangular region on the source surface can be copied into a rectangle on the destination surface. Though surfaces can be copied, none are visible on the screen except the main window surface, which was created by the **SDL_SetVideoMode** function. Surfaces copied to the main window, therefore, will draw their contents on screen; this is how images are made visible using SDL. Surfaces are copied using the SDL_BlitSurface function.

The main window surface will be cleared (erased, or refreshed) on each frame of the game loop. Therefore, surfaces should be blitted to the main window on each frame; not just once. This is useful because the position of a surface when blitted to the window could be changed over time to create an animation.

```
int SDL_BlitSurface(SDL_Surface *src, SDL_Rect
   *srcrect, SDL_Surface *dst, SDL_Rect *dstrect);
```

Argument List

src – pointer to a valid source surface.

srcrect – pointer to a source *rect*. This can be NULL if you intend to copy the whole of the source surface, or a pointer to a *rect* structure defining a region on the source surface to copy.

dst – pointer to a valid destination surface.

dstrect – pointer to a destination *rect*. Like the source *rect*, this can be NULL to copy to the top left corner of the *dst*, or a pointer to a rectangular region inside which to paste.

Sample code

```
SDL_Rect SourceRct;
SourceRct.x = 0; SourceRct.w = 100;
SourceRct.y= 0; SourceRct.h = 100;
```

```
SDL_Rect DestRct;
DestRct.x = 50; DestRct.w = 100;
DestRct.y = 50; DestRct.h = 100;

//Copies from the top left of the source surface,
//100 pixels by 100 pixels wide to the dest
//(Screen) at position (50,50). Measured from top
//left corner.

SDL_BlitSurface(MySurface, &SourceRct, screen,
  &DestRct);
```

Filling and clearing surfaces

A surface can be filled with a specific colour using the *SDL_FillRect* function. This is useful if you want to clean a surface of its contents. It should also be used to clean the main window surface at the start of each frame.

```
int SDL_FillRect(SDL_Surface *dst, SDL_Rect
  *dstrect, Uint32 color);
```

Argument list

dst – surface to fill.

dstrect – this can be NULL, to fill the whole surface, or a pointer to an SDL_Rect structure to fill a specified rectangle.

Color – the colour to fill. It is a numerical RGB colour value. To specify colours in SDL, the function SDL_MapRGB can be used. It accepts as arguments the pixel format to use, and the red, blue and green colour components.

Sample code

```
// clear screen
  SDL_FillRect(screen, 0, SDL_MapRGB(screen->
  format, 0, 0, 0));
```

Surface colour keying

The Sokoban game will include a variety of tiles – boxes, walls, floors and so on, but none of them need *colour keying* except for the player tile. This is called a *sprite* because it will be animated, but it has another important property – its background colour should be transparent. As the player image is overlaid onto the level, players will not expect its solid square borders to be visible. Instead, they will expect to see the player seamlessly in the level. There are two main ways of making colours transparent in games; one is through alpha blending (not covered in this book), and the other is via colour keying. Colour keying works by making one specific colour in the image excluded, so that any pixels that match the colour key will not be drawn, and nor will they be copied to other surfaces during blitting. This implies the background colour should be unique in the image so it will be the only set of pixels to become transparent. A colour key can be applied to a surface using the *SDL_SetColorKey* function.

```
int SDL_SetColorKey(SDL_Surface *surface, Uint32
  flag, Uint32 key);
```

Argument list

surface – pointer to a valid source surface.

flag – this should be SDL_SRCCOLORKEY to indicate that the argument key specifies the colour key. This flag can also be Or'd with flag SDL_RLEACCEL to enable Run Length Encoding (RLE). This flag will speed up the process of colour keying.

key – a RGB color to be the colour key.

Sample code

```
SDL_SetColorKey(MySurface, SDL_SRCCOLORKEY |
  SDL_RLEACCEL, m_ColourKey);
```

4.8 Drawing in the game loop

To complete this chapter, it is necessary to return to the game loop and see a practical example of SDL blitting on the window surface during a frame, an iteration of the game loop. Each frame requires a game to clear the main surface, blit whatever game graphics need to be blitted, and then to end the frame. Consider the following game loop which blits a previously loaded surface to the window.

Figure 4.1 An image blitted to the screen

```
bool done = false;
while (!done)
{
  // message processing loop
  SDL_Event event;
  while (SDL_PollEvent(&event))
  {
    // check for messages
    //...
  } // end of message processing

  // DRAWING STARTS HERE
  // clear screen
  SDL_FillRect(screen,0,SDL_MapRGB(screen->
  format, 0, 0, 0));

  //Draw image here
  //SDL_BlitSurface(bmp, 0, screen, 0);

  //End Frame
  SDL_Flip(screen);

} // end main loop
```

Notice each frame ends with a call to **SDL_Flip**. This function accepts a valid surface as an argument. In almost all cases this argument will be the main surface. In effect, this function ends a frame. It confirms to SDL that all blits to the main surface for this frame are completed. Blits to the main surface will not become visible until SDL_Flip is called.

Page flipping

SDL_Flip works by a process called page flipping. Behind the scenes, SDL keeps two surfaces for the window: the front buffer and the back buffer. The front buffer holds what is currently visible on the screen. During a frame as other surfaces are blitted to the main surface, the changes are accumulated on the back buffer. When SDL_Flip is called, the buffers swap places. The back buffer becomes the front buffer and its contents are drawn to the display, and the front buffer becomes the back where it will be drawn to on the next frame.

Summary

This chapter explained how to draw graphics with the SDL. These functions and processes are essential for the Sokoban game and will later be used to draw its levels. The SDL can be seen as a simple, fast and effective library for games, because it offers intuitive mechanisms for blitting images to the display. A surface encapsulates an image, and colour keying ensures certain parts of images can be made transparent.

Before proceeding, it will be useful to take some time out and play around with SDL. For example, try blitting a series of surfaces onto the main surface and think about how the order of blitting affects the results.

05 audio programming

In this chapter you will learn about:

- sound and music
- MP3, WAV and OGG
- audio software
- BASS audio library
- playing streams

Music is the application of sounds to the canvas of silence.

Carl Jung

5.1 Defining audio

On an old British TV game show (*You Bet*), a boy accepted the challenge to identify any computer game by listening to a few seconds of its soundtrack. He succeeded. But even if he hadn't his attempt would still have been testament to the importance of audio. For computer games, audio has far-reaching effects; more than just setting an atmosphere and sounding fun, it is important for making games accessible to people with disabilities.

Audio has a comparatively short history in computer games. It was only around 10 years ago that sound cards became an essential component for a PC. First appearing in the 1970s, sound for games was monotone and somewhat dull. Later, inventive kinds of sound systems emerged – like pulse code modulation (PCM) which was part of consoles like the Super Nintendo and Sega Megadrive. Since then CD audio and streamable formats like MP3 and OGG have supplanted all the older types. For computer games audio has two forms, sound and music.

Sound

A sound is a noise; like a tap drip or a foot step. Unlike music, which may last for minutes, sounds usually last no more than 30 seconds. For example, in some games, guns fire a series of rounds for a long time. During this time the noise is relentless. But it is not really continuous. The game simply repeats a short sound for as long as needed. Sounds also provide important feedback to the player, making instructive noises when the player performs certain actions. Completing a level might play a high-toned congratulations noise. On the other hand, defeat will cause a slower, negative noise to be heard. In either case, no text or image needs to be shown in order to convey the mood. In this case, the sound has given feedback.

Music

Music is often referred to as *BGM* (*BackGround Music*). It is all the tracks featured in a game. Sometimes they are songs, sometimes instrumental, and sometimes they are just atmospheric. These tend to be one long composition of sounds, like the wind howling, dogs barking and police sirens. It isn't strictly music because there is no rhythm or lyrics. But, it's a continuous piece of sound, and in this sense is classified as music. There is also *incidental music*, which refers to a collection of tracks that merge into one another according to the mood of the game. It might begin in a peaceful mood with a calm track. But as an enemy fires, the music changes into an intense heart thumping beat. Our game of Sokoban will consider standard BGM only.

Audio formats

Game audio can be in a number of different file formats, including MP3, WAV and OGG. The quality of sound varies between them and some formats are more common than others. Sokoban will be able to play music from most common formats including those just listed. These are considered in more detail below.

- **MP3** (MPEG-1 Audio Layer 3) – came to prominence in 1996 and is now the most common music format. These days, nearly everybody has heard of MP3. Despite being popular, MP3 has a number of limitations. It has technical limitations, such as a capped bit rate of 320kbits per second, and there are patent issues – developers cannot legally distribute MP3 encoders or decoders unless they pay a licence fee.

- **WAV** (Wave format) – the most typical kind of WAV file is uncompressed audio stored in a pulse code modulation format. WAV files tend to be very large for longer chunks of audio, but being uncompressed, their quality is good. For this reason, they are commonly used for sound effects in games.

- **OGG** – an exciting new alternative to MP3. This is a patent-free format developed by Vorbis. It overcomes many of the technical limitations of MP3 and is free to use. At the time of writing OGG is not as widely supported as MP3, but the BASS audio library considered later in this chapter offers the power to play audio in many formats, including OGG.

5.2 Making music

Before programming sound with BASS, it's useful to consider how audio is created for games. Sound effects are either recorded or purchased on large compilation CDs. Sound can be recorded using software like Audacity or Sound Forge. But what about music? And what happens if, like me, you're not musically talented? This section briefly examines the facilities and software available for music.

Hiring musicians and bands

Many big games companies hire established artists to make music for their games, and the artists usually charge per minute of music. However, for independent developers and newcomers it doesn't always work this way. The world is full of new artists and bands looking to get their music heard. In fact, computer games are a remarkably useful medium for fledgling artists to make their mark. So for the new games developer starting out, there is an incentive for both parties to work together. For this reason, smaller game teams often featured music made by independent artists, and often the cost this incurs is surprisingly small.

Buy out music

This is also called royalty-free music. These are songs already recorded and featured on compilation albums. You pay an initial fee to buy the album, and it grants you the right to use the music for films, or games, or whatever you choose. This method of purchasing music is more common for TV programmes and for use at public venues, but is less common for games.

Making your own

Making music is a diverse field. Some people have or can hire the facilities to record their own songs, and others make music on the computer. For the latter option, there's a wide selection of software available. This includes: eJay, Fruity Loops, Rebirth and Cubase. Check the References section (page 180) to find more information on Internet sources.

5.3 BASS audio

Let's look now at audio programming, in the context of Sokoban. The library to be used for this will be the BASS audio library, an easy-to-use and comprehensive suite of classes and functions. BASS is cross-platform, widely documented and free for non-commercial use. Commercial games entail a licence fee but (at the time of writing) discounts are available for independent developers and small teams. This makes BASS one of the most popular audio libraries around.

BASS can play audio in these formats: WAV, AIFF, MP3, MP2, MP1, OGG, CDA, MO3, IT, XM, S3M, MTM, MOD, UMX.

Downloading and configuring BASS

BASS is quick and easy to download. The download package (from **http://www.un4seen.com/**) includes the runtime library, the development libraries and documentation. As with SDL, the development libraries do not need to be distributed with your applications – only the runtime package, which in this case, consists of only bass.dll. This should be installed in the same folder as the game's executable file.

Configuring BASS for Visual C++

To use BASS in Visual C++, its library files should either be copied into the existing lib and include directories for VC++, or else new directories should be added to the compiler search list.

To configure BASS:

1. Create a new project or open an existing project. This can be any kind of Windows project.

2. Click **Project > Properties**. This opens the Project Properties dialog box where you can specify project settings. For more information see Chapter 3.

3. Click **C/C++**.

4. In the **Additional Include Directories** edit box, add the BASS\C directory. This is the *include* directory.

5. In the list box, click **Linker**. In the **Additional Library Directories**, add BASS\C. This should be the directory containing BASS.lib.

6   In **Linker/Input**, add "bass.lib" to the additional dependencies edit box. This will tell the C++ compiler to link to the BASS.lib file. The project is now ready to use.

Configuring BASS for Code::Blocks

Code::Blocks does not feature a wizard for BASS like it does for SDL. Therefore, it will need to be configured manually:

1   Create a new project or open an existing project. This can be any kind of Windows project.

2   Click **Project > Build Options**. This opens the Project Options dialog box where you can specify project settings. (For more information, refer back to Chapter 3.)

3   Click the **Directories** tab.

4   In the **Directories/Compiler** tab, add the BASS\C directory. This is the Include directory.

5   In the **Directories/Linker** tab, add BASS\C. This should be the directory containing BASS.lib.

6   Click the **Linker** tab, click **Add** to add the BASS.lib file. The project is now ready to use.

5.4   Programming with BASS

Having configured an IDE to use the BASS library, a BASS application can then be created. Using BASS, a game will be able to play all sorts of audio files, and advanced features like surround sound and 3D sound are available for suitable sound cards. In the context of Sokoban, BASS will be used to play BGM (Background Music) while the player attempts to solve a level.

NOTE. All BASS applications should include the BASS header file #include<BASS.h>.

Initializing BASS

BASS applications begin by calling the function, **BASS_Init**. This initializes the library for playing sound, and performs a number of checks. BASS determines the sound hardware such as the kind of card on the system, and whether one is present at all. No other BASS function can be called successfully before BASS_Init.

It must return TRUE, for BASS applications to continue. If it returns FALSE, then no sound can be played using BASS. The function accepts a number of arguments. Its prototype is:

```
BOOL BASS_Init(
    int device,
    DWORD freq,
    DWORD flags,
    HWND win,
    GUID *clsid
);
```

Argument list

device – indicates the sound card to use. A system may have more than one sound card installed. -1 specifies the default and 0 specifies no sound. Sokoban will use -1, and most applications are likely to select this. **BASS_GetDeviceDescription** can be used to determine whether a sound device is associated with a specified number. If so, its number can be passed as this argument.

freq – the output sample rate in Hz of the sound. The most common value for stereo sound is 44,100 Hz.

flags – this will be 0 unless an application has a specific requirement. For example, BASS_DEVICE_3D can be passed if 3D sound should be enabled. Or, BASS_DEVICE_MONO can be passed to play sound in mono. Sokoban will accept the defaults and pass 0. A complete list of the flags for this argument can be found in the BASS documentation.

win – associates the BASS library with a window. This can be NULL to associate BASS with the active application window.

clsid – This should be NULL.

Sample code

```
//Initializethe default device; 44100hz stereo
//16-bits
if (!BASS_Init(-1,44100,0,NULL,NULL))
{
    // couldn't initialize device, so "no sound"
    BASS_Init(0,44100,0,hwnd,NULL);
}
```

A call to **BASS_Init** should be coupled with a call to **BASS_Free** to close the library. This typically is called at the end of an application.

Retrieving device information

Given the number of a sound device, BASS can return hardware information about it, such as the number of speakers it supports, the amount of memory of the device, and so on. This is encoded into a BASS_INFO struct, and can be returned from a call to **BASS_GetInfo**. A complete list of members for this structure can be found in the BASS documentation, but some of the most useful are:

hwsize – the amount of memory of the hardware device.

hwfree – how much of that total is available.

minrate – the minimum sample rate.

maxrate – the maximum sample rate supported by the hardware. Therefore, the BASS_Init sample rate can be any value between and including these.

speakers – the number of speakers the device supports.

Common device operations

BASS offers a number of functions to control the sound card, which can be thought of as master controls. It is possible to start and stop playback and to set the volume for individual sound. The following functions apply to the sound device overall, and not specific sounds. These settings will apply to all sounds played using the sound device.

BASS_GetVolume and BASS_SetVolume

The master volume can range between 0 (min) and 100 (max), e.g. BASS_SetVolume(50);

BASS_Start, BASS_Stop, BASS_Pause

Each of these functions accept no arguments. They start, stop and pause master playback respectively.

BASS_ErrorGetCode

This function returns an integer describing the most recent error, if any, that BASS encountered.

5.5 Samples and streams

To encapsulate audio, BASS distinguishes between *samples* and *streams*. Though this is technically based, as we shall see, it is analogous to the distinction between sound and music. BASS has a class for each of the sample and stream types. Both classes can be played over the speakers using class *Channel*, so all the Channel related functions of BASS can be used and applied transparently to both samples and streams. The Channel class and playback is considered later (see page 73). This section explores how to load different sounds using BASS.

Samples and BASS

Typically, samples are short, periodic WAV sounds. They are likely to be used frequently in an application, and for this reason, are fully loaded into memory. A number of special effects can also be applied to them; like 3D positioning and surround sound. To represent a sample, BASS uses a HSAMPLE object. Sounds are loaded from audio files using the **BASS_SampleLoad** function. This accepts a valid filename and returns a HSAMPLE object to the newly loaded sample. If an error occurred, the return value will be 0 and the error code can be retrieved using **BASS_ErrorGetCode**. Consider the following:

```
HSAMPLE BASS_SampleLoad(
  BOOL mem,
  void *file,
  DWORD offset,
  DWORD length,
  DWORD max,
  DWORD flags
);
```

This function does not start playback of the sound, but simply loads it into memory.

Argument list

mem – should be TRUE if loading from files. Sounds can be loaded from memory. This topic is not considered in this book.

file – the filename of the sound to be loaded. Note, the std::string objects can be converted to const char* (see page 41).

offset – should be 0 when loading from files.

length – should be 0 when loading from files.

max – can be used to set the maximum number of simultaneous playbacks allowed for this sample; 1 (min) or 65,535 (max). For example, if a game featured a house with locked doors that made a knocking sound every time the player clicked on them, a max limit would need to be set. As the player clicks, the knocking begins to indicate the door is locked. The sound is initiated and the player is given back the cursor. However, the knocking sound hasn't finished. What happens if the player clicks again while the sound is still playing? Should another instance of the knocking sound begin, so that two overlapping knocks would be heard? Probably not. Better is to set the max limit to 1. This way, only one instance of the sound is playing at any one time.

flags – can be different values which specify how the sample is to be loaded and played. The only value considered here is BASS_SAMPLE_LOOP. This flag, if set, tells the sound to continually loop. If it is played, then it will continue to play over and over again until it is manually stopped.

Sample code

```
HSTREAM Stream = BASS_SampleLoad(true,
  filename.c_str(),0,0,1,BASS_SAMPLE_LOOP);
```

For every successful call to **BASS_SampleLoad** there should be a corresponding call to **BASS_SampleFree**. This frees up memory when the sound is no longer needed.

Streams and BASS

A stream is a song, a soundtrack, or some longer piece of sound. It corresponds to MP3s and OGG files. Unlike samples, streams are not entirely loaded into memory. Instead, the files are *streamed*, i.e. they're loaded a portion at a time corresponding to the part being played. This keeps memory usage to a minimum, but it increases the overhead and reduces the number of effects that can be applied to it. Streams are represented by the HSTREAM class. They can be loaded from files using the **BASS_StreamCreateFile**.

```
HSTREAM BASS_StreamCreateFile(
  BOOL mem,
  void *file,
  DWORD offset,
  DWORD length,
  DWORD flags
);
```

Argument list

mem – should be TRUE if loading from files.

file – the filename to the sound to be loaded.

offset – should be 0 when loading from files.

length – should be 0 when loading from files.

flags – see the definition for **BASS_SampleLoad** (page 71).

Sample code

```
HSTREAM Stream=BASS_StreamCreateFile(FALSE,
  Filename.c_str(),0,0,0)
```

For every call to **BASS_StreamCreateFile** there should be a corresponding call to **BASS_StreamFree**. This will free the stream object from memory.

5.6 Channels

Neither samples nor streams are played upon loading. Instead, a series of channel functions are used to control their playback. A channel represents a sample or a stream that can be played. Using channels, playback of samples and streams can be started, stopped, paused, and so on.

Playing channels

Channels are loaded with samples or streams, and can be played back. To load and play a channel, the **BASS_ChannelPlay** function can be called. The method of playback differs a little depending on whether a sample or stream is being played. First, the function prototype for BASS_ChannelPlay is considered.

```
BOOL BASS_ChannelPlay(
  DWORD handle,
  BOOL restart
);
```

Argument list

handle – the channel object to play. For streams this will be the actual object (HSTREAM); for samples, it will be the channel object returned from BASS_SampleGetChannel. This function accepts two arguments; the sample for which to get a channel, and a TRUE/FALSE value to determine whether it should be assigned a new channel. This value will nearly always be FALSE.

Restart – a true/false value to determine whether playback should resume from the beginning. If the channel was previously paused, you may want playback to resume from where it was paused (false), or else (true) playback starts from the beginning.

Sample code for streams

```
BASS_ChannelPlay(Stream, true);
```

Sample code for samples

```
HCHANNEL Chl = BASS_SampleGetChannel(Str, false);
BASS_ChannelPlay(Chl, false);
```

Using channels

Besides playing audio via channels, there are a number of other functions related to channels and audio playback. These include:

BASS_ChannelStop

Stops channel playback. This differs from pause since it flushes the channel, meaning playback will resume at the beginning. Example: **BASS_ChannelStop(myChannel);**

BASS_ChannelPause

Pauses a channel. To resume use **BASS_ChannelPlay**.

BASS_ChannelActive

This function can be used to determine whether a specified channel is currently playing. Calling this function will return one of the following state values:

```
BASS_ACTIVE_STOPPED
BASS_ACTIVE_PLAYING
BASS_ACTIVE_PAUSED
```

BASS_ChannelSetPosition

Used to set the position of playback. Measured as an offset of the number of bytes from the beginning of the stream. Example:
BASS_ChannelSetPosition(myChannel, 100);

Summary

This chapter concludes part of a broader section of this book. It has looked at audio in games programming, using libraries. On its own, BASS is a comprehensive and exciting library, not least because of the file format support it offers. It supports MP3, OGG, WAV and many more. But BASS is also interesting because it controls the sound hardware at a high level, making it fast and painless to use. Further to its efficiency and like SDL, BASS only requires a small runtime DLL to be distributed with its applications, making BASS an excellent choice for game sound.

06

game mechanics

In this chapter you will learn about:

- scene management
- resources
- sprites and tiles
- input and response
- game engine
- painter's algorithm

*I must create a system or be enslaved by another man's. I
will not reason and compare ... my business is to create.*

William Blake

6.1 Making Sokoban

Up until now the design, programming, graphics and sound have
been considered in isolation. They have been examined as being
smaller parts of a complete Sokoban game. Code::Blocks or VC++
was used as an IDE. SDL was chosen for graphics, and BASS
was selected for sound. Naturally, these are each important aspects of a game, but it's important to look at how these libraries
come together to make a full game of Sokoban.

When thinking about how to make Sokoban, and most other
games, it's a good idea to think abstractly and see the game in
terms of larger parts. Accepting SDL will be used for graphics,
and BASS will be used for sound, these will form larger units.
For example, there needs to be a component that processes and
draws levels. There needs to be a system of input. There needs to
be a module for loading and playing sounds on demand. Higher
still, encompassing all of these components is the *game engine*.
This chapter is concerned with creating the game engine, which
is made up of the following parts.

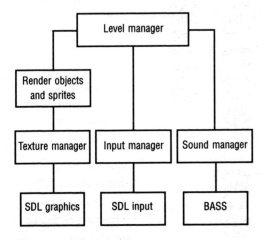

Figure 6.1 Summary of Sokoban

Resources

Sokoban makes use of two main resources: graphics and sound. It needs to load in image files for the level tiles and player sprite, and to stream in music for the BGM. Each graphic or sound is a resource and the game must manage them. This involves creating resources from files and deleting them from memory when they're no longer needed. Sokoban will have a dedicated resource manager component for creating and deleting resources.

Level manager

Sokoban uses a system of image tiles to create levels, and needs a dedicated level manager to load its levels. This manager must build the grid and draw it to the screen. It's also responsible for managing the positions of movable items, such as boxes and the player, and for checking to see if the level is won.

Render manager

Aside from the level itself, there may be other things that will appear on the screen during the game. This might be a high score, a 'level-complete' screen, an error message, or an options menu. Typically, these displays will appear on the foreground where the player can see them above everything else. Hence, there needs to be a component which manages the order in which things are drawn. This is called the render manager.

Input manager

To play Sokoban the player presses keys to move the character and interact with the game world. The Up, Down, Left and Right arrows move the character respectively, and [R] will restart a level. To process key presses and ensure these are mapped to appropriate game actions, an input manager will be created.

6.2 Resources – texture manager

In game terminology, images like BMPs and JPGs are called *textures*. Keep in mind textures will be loaded using SDL. Sokoban will need to use many textures, such as the level tiles and other images. Some of them will be independent single tile textures, and others will be tileable. That is, textures with different images on them arranged in equal tiles. Games can handle textures in many ways. The best way is to use a texture manager.

TIP. The worst way to handle textures is to load them each time they are needed, haphazardly anywhere in code, not bothering to keep track of the loaded items. First, this leads to memory leakages, duplicate textures floating around in memory, and difficulty keeping track of what's been loaded and what has not. And what happens if later on you decide to change the graphics library? Instead of using SDL, you want to convert to OpenGL? You would need to scan through every line of code searching for lines of SDL to replace with OpenGL equivalents. Creating a centralized class to handle textures keeps the code organized and in one place, as the next section shows.

Creating the texture manager

The texture manager is a centralized class that handles textures. It is called when a texture needs to be created. It's responsible for maintaining a list of textures and does this by keeping track of all SDL_Surface pointers (see 4.7 *SDL surfaces*). It's also responsible for deleting textures from memory when appropriate. There should be no occasion when a texture is created without calling the texture manager. This avoids duplication – if the manager is called upon to create a duplicate, it simply returns a pointer to the existing texture. Consider this texture manager class.

```
//Texture Manager Class to load and manage
  textures
class cTextureManager
{
  public:
  //List of textures
  std::vector<SDL_Surface*> m_Surfaces;
  //Destructor
  ~cTextureManager()
  {
    //Clear the list
    for (unsigned int indx = 0; indx <
      m_Surfaces.size(); indx++)
      SDL_FreeSurface(m_Surfaces[indx]);
  }
```

```
//Loads a new texture
SDL_Surface* loadSurface(std::string Filename)
{
  SDL_Surface*Tmp =
    SDL_LoadBMP(Filename.c_str());
  SDL_Surface* bmp = NULL;

  if(Tmp)
  {
    bmp = SDL_DisplayFormat(Tmp);
    SDL_FreeSurface(Tmp);

    //Add to list
    if(bmp)
      m_Surfaces.push_back(bmp);
  }
  return bmp;
}
};
```

Comments

- **loadSurface** adds a new texture to the list. It returns a pointer to the newly created texture. This can be used by any other classes and functions as required, but it is the job of the manager to delete the pointer.

- **loadSurface** uses SDL_DisplayFormat to optimize the surface.

- The texture manager uses a std::vector class to manage the texture list (see Chapter 3).

> It's helpful to organize classes into separate source and header files. This makes your code easier to read.

6.3 Base classes and managers

Sokoban has other managers, and the most important of these are the render manager, input manager and level manager. The render manager is responsible for drawing items to the screen; the input manager makes sure user input is passed onto the appropriate sections, like the level manager.

In any game there could be a variety of different objects that need to be drawn and an equally large variety that need input. In Sokoban, the level manager needs input so it can process where the player is and where they are moving to. Additionally, it needs to be drawn to the screen, to show the level. Other objects, like a 'level complete' screen also need to be drawn and need input. This screen might say 'Press any key to continue', and so needs to know about that key press.

There could be many classes that want input and to be drawn even though the implementation of those classes may differ greatly. For this reason, the render manager and input manager will assume all such classes are derived from a common ancestor class, an abstract base class. Due to polymorphism, this means all derived classes can be notified about drawing and input events by the managers through virtual functions.

Virtual functions

In object orientated programming, virtual functions are those which can be overridden in descendant classes. If a method of the base class is called, it will invoke the overridden version in the descendant class. Polymorphism means that derived classes are type safe with their ancestor class. This allows derived objects to be passed to functions accepting their base classes.

Creating the base class

The base class will be called *cRenderObject*. Its purpose is to be a base class for any object that needs to receive input and/or to be drawn on screen. As a result, the level manager will be derived from this class, so will any kind of 'level complete' screen, and so on. The base class cannot be instantiated directly, but classes should be derived from it. It will expose several virtual methods, all of which should be overridden in descendant classes. These are: the update method, an input method and a virtual destructor. The update method will be called on each frame of the game loop to notify the system that the class needs to be drawn. Likewise, the input method is called each time user input occurs. Finally, the virtual destructor makes sure the destructor is called in descendant classes when the object is deleted.

Consider the following code.

```cpp
//Base class for all renderable objects
class cRenderObject
{
  public:
  std::string m_Name; //User defined name
  int m_ZOrder;
  bool m_Visible;

  cRenderObject(std::string Name)
  {
    m_Name = Name;
    m_ZOrder = 0;
    m_Visible = true;
  }

  virtual ~cRenderObject(){};
  //Class virtual destructor
  //method to draw
  virtual void update(SDL_Surface *Screen) = 0;
  //method for input
  virtual bool updateKey(SDLKey Key) = 0;
};
```

Comments

* **update** is called when drawing needs to happen. It accepts a surface argument. This should be a pointer to the screen surface, or any surface destination where drawing should occur. This is useful because it means you can draw the entire object to surfaces other than the screen if required.

* **m_Visible** is a flag to determine the visibility of an object. The render and input Managers will ignore processing any object if this flag is false.

* **m_Name** is an optional member. It is for a programmer's reference. It can be any string, preferably a descriptive one.

The render manager

In the previous subsection, the base class cRenderObject was created. This class is the starting point for any object wanting to be drawn or to receive input. The job of the render manager is to keep a list of cRenderObjects and make sure they're drawn to the screen on every frame. This list will include at least the level manager and may also include other objects, such as a level complete screen. Any object on the list will be called on each frame for drawing. The render manager class may look like this:

```
class cRenderManager
{
  public:
  //List of objects to draw on screen
  std::vector<cRenderObject*> m_Objects;

  //Draws child objects, called each frame
  void update()
  {
    //Loop through objects
    for (unsigned int indx = 0; indx <
      m_Objects.size(); indx++)
    {
      if(m_Objects[indx]->m_Visible)
        m_Objects[indx]->update(screen);
    }
  }
  void addRenderObject(cRenderObject* Object)
  {
    m_Objects.push_back(Object);
  }
};
```

Comments

• Unlike the texture manager, the render manager is not responsible for deleting render objects. This is because they may have more transient and specific lifetimes. So other functions and classes are responsible for deleting them.

• The **update** method of the render manager should be called on each frame. This in turn calls the update method of each render object in the list for you. Notice how it passes the SDL screen surface to each object as an argument.

• **addRenderObject** adds a render object to the list. The list of renderobjects is handled by std::vector class.

The painter's algorithm

Though it will not generally apply to Sokoban since it is a tile-based game, there is a consideration for a render manager that should be noted – the order of render objects in the list. If more than one object is drawn on a frame, when a surface is copied to the screen it will be drawn over the top of any previously drawn surfaces. This is the Z order. It means that objects in the distance (background objects) should be drawn first and foreground surfaces drawn afterwards. The nearer an object is to the camera, the later it features in the list. This technique is known as the Painter's Algorithm. Its purpose is to make sure objects appear as they would in real life.

The input manager

Unlike the render manager, the input manager does not process input on every frame. Instead, it is called to action only on key press events. When one occurs, the manager cycles through its list of render objects to pass the event onto. Input will be intended for only one object. So the first render object to return TRUE during the cycle will be the target for input and no further objects in the queue will receive the key press for this event. This is to make sure unexpected behaviour doesn't happen for later objects in the list. For example, the level complete screen says 'Press any key to continue'. If the player presses the right arrow key, we expect the screen to disappear and move on to the next level. But we do not expect the player to move right while that screen is still active. For this reason, input is intended for one object, and this object will be the first to 'eat' it. As with the render manager, the order of input is important and is related to Z order, but the order of input is the inverse of render order. So the first item to be drawn (the item at the back) will be the last to receive input, and the last item to be drawn will be the first to receive input. Consider the following code.

```
class cInputManager
{
  public:
  std::vector<cRenderObject*> m_InputObjects;
```

```
void updateKey(SDLKey Key)
{
  for(unsigned int indx =
    m_InputObjects.size()-1; indx >= 0; indx-)
  {
    if(m_InputObjects[indx]->m_Visible)
    if(m_InputObjects[indx]->updateKey(Key))
    return;
  }
}
void addInputObject(cRenderObject *Object)
{
  m_InputObjects.push_back(Object);
};
};
```

Comments

- **updateKey** accepts an SDL_Key code for the pressed key and returns if a key is eaten.

- **addInputObject** adds an object to the list.

6.4 Sprites

A *sprite* is an animated texture, that is, a series of textures or tiles played in a consecutive sequence over time, just like a flick book cartoon. For Sokoban there will be only one sprite, which will be for the player. It will have two frames, tiles of equal width and equal height, and they will be played repeatedly, looping over and over again – even when the player moves boxes around. The animation is an excited movement – flapping arms.

Figure 6.2 Player sprite

A sprite has a position in terms of (x,y), measured relative to the top left corner of the screen. Consider this class declaration.

```
class cSprite : public cRenderObject
{
  protected:
    SDL_Surface *m_SpriteSurface;
    int m_FrameCount;
    bool m_Playing;
  public:
    int m_FPS;
    int m_CurrentFrame;
    int m_XPos;
    int m_YPos;

  cSprite(std::string Name, int FrameCount);
  ~cSprite();

  //Overloaded virtual draw
  void update(SDL_Surface *Screen);
  bool updateKey(SDLKey Key);
  SDL_Surface*loadSprite(std::string Filename,
  bool enableColourKey=false,int colourKey=0);
};
```

Comments

- **m_SpriteSurface** is the texture to be used for the Sprite.

- The sprite will support colour keying (see Chapter 4).

- **m_Playing** reflects whether the sprite is currently animated.

Animating with time

A sprite is simply a specialized texture. Given a texture with several tiles, the sprite's job is to show only one tile per frame. Changing the tile creates animation. Time is important as it is used to specify when events occur in an animation, when frame changes happen and the speed at which objects move, measured in milliseconds (1000 = 1 second) or frames per second. If you wanted an object to move across the screen at 50 pixels per second, and decided to show two frames per second, the movement would be 25 pixels each time. There are many functions which can be used to measure time.

The following code is called on every frame. It uses the SDL library to measure time, and does this by keeping track of each passing second. It also generates a scalar value (between 0 and 1) to indicate what proportion of a second has passed, where 1 means a whole second has elapsed, 0 means a new second has begun, and 0.5 means half a second passed. This can be used to determine which frame of the sprite should be shown.

Frame-based animation

Some older games neglected time. Instead, they animated sprites and objects based on each frame. Literally taking every passing frame of the game loop to represent a frame of animation. The problem was that performance varied from machine to machine. Some went through more iterations than others in the same amount of time, so that faster machines did more iterations of the game loop per second than slower ones. Different gamers had different experiences depending on their machines. This led to confused animations, bad synchronization, and annoyed customers.

```
//SDL_GetTicks() returns the number of
//milliseconds since SDL was initialized.
//StartTime was initialized to SDL_GetTicks()
//when the animation began. StartTime is also
//re-initialized to SDL_GetTicks() at the
//beginning of each second.

//Number of milliseconds elapsed
CurrentTime = SDL_GetTicks() - StartTime;
//Has a second elapsed?
if(CurrentTime >= 1000)
{
  //If yes, then begin new second
  StartTime = SDL_GetTicks();
  CurrentTime = 0;
  return;
}
//Else
  //Generate scalar (floating point value between
  //0 and 1)
  float Scalar = CurrentTime / 1000.0f;
```

```
//Calculate frame to show, e.g. if FPS = 30 and
//Scalar = 0.5 Current Frame will be 15
float Frame = Scalar * FPS;
```

Creating the sprite

If the sprite needs to show frame 0 (the first), how does it know where to find this on the texture? How does it know which pixel positions correspond to frame 0? The player sprite is a texture with two tiles, each 50 pixels wide and 50 pixels high, arranged in a row of two columns. The top left corner of Tile 0 is at (0,0) and the top left corner of Tile 1 is at (50,0). Remember from Chapter 4 that SDL can draw a specified rectangle of pixels from a surface. Therefore, as time passes, the rectangle will change between Tile 0 and Tile 1. Consider the following sample code.

```
//CurrentFrame = 0 or 1
//Size = 50 pixels

  SDL_Rect SourceRct;
  SourceRct.x = CurrentFrame * Size; SourceRct.w
    = Size;
  SourceRct.y = 0; SourceRct.h = Size;

  SDL_Rect DestRect;
  DestRect.x = XPos; DestRect.w = Size;
  DestRect.y = YPos; DestRect.h = Size;

  SDL_BlitSurface(SpriteSurface, &SourceRct,
    Screen, &DestRect);
```

6.5 Levels

A Sokoban level consists of the player, a series of boxes and destination squares, walls and the floor. The level is tile-based, with a grid where every square is of equal size. In this sense, the level works like a two dimensional array. In our game, a Sokoban level is no larger than 20 squares by 20 squares, and each square is 50 pixels wide by 50 pixels high. In practice, Sokoban keeps track of two grids. They are both the same size, and have a 1:1 correspondence in terms of positions. One grid represents the static level, including the walls, floors and destination squares; a second grid keeps track of the position of the movable objects – the player and boxes.

Drawing levels

The static grid is associated with a texture, which includes all the tiles that can appear in it. There is 0 = floor , 1 = wall and 2 = destination square tile. Any element in the array can be 0, 1 or 2 depending on which tile that square should be. Drawing the level, involves cycling through the array and drawing each tile. The previous section demonstrated how a specific tile can be drawn from the texture using the SDL rectangles, based on whether it should draw the first tile, second or third, and so on.

Like the static grid, the movable grid is also associated with textures, namely the player sprite and boxes. This is drawn in the same way as the static grid.

```
for(int indx1 = 0; indx1 < 20; indx1++)
  for(int indx2 = 0; indx2 < 20; indx2++)
  {
    int Index =
      m_CurrentLevel.m_Level[indx1][indx2];

    SDL_Rect SourceRct;
    SourceRct.x = Index * TileSize; SourceRct.w =
      TileSize;
    SourceRct.y= 0; SourceRct.h = TileSize;

    SDL_Rect DestRct;
    DestRct.x = indx2 * TileSize; DestRct.w =
      TileSize;
    DestRct.y = indx1 * TileSize; DestRct.h =
      TileSize;
    SDL_BlitSurface(LevelTiles, &SourceRct,
      Screen, &DestRct);
}
```

Checking for a win

The player can win on any move. In our implementation, a winning condition is where for each destination element in the static array, the corresponding element in the movable array is occupied by a box, i.e. there is a box on every destination square. The following code will check for a win.

```
bool checkForWin()
{
  for(int indx1 = 0; indx1 < 20; indx1++)
    for(int indx2 = 0; indx2 < 20; indx2++)
    {
      int Index =
        m_CurrentLevel.m_Level[indx1][indx2];

      if(Index == OBJECT_DEST)
        if(m_CurrentLevel.m_MovArray[indx1]
          [indx2] != OBJECT_BOX)
        return false;
    }
    return true;
}
```

Process level input

A key press signifies user input. Acceptable presses are **[R]** for restarting the level, and the arrow keys for character movement. All other key presses are ignored except **[Esc]** for exiting. On each valid key press a number of steps must be taken:

*   **[Esc]** – exit game.

*   **[R]** – the level must be reset to its original condition; end of input processing.

*   If an arrow key was pressed it needs to be considered further.

    *   The player cannot move if there is a wall on the neighbouring space in that direction.

    *   The player can move if there is a neighbouring vacant space in that direction.

    *   The player cannot move if there is a box in the indicated direction *and* if there is a wall or box beyond it – you cannot push two boxes at once, or push a box through a wall.

    *   The player and box can move if there is a box next to the player in that direction, and the space beyond is vacant.

Sample code

This processes user input.

```
bool doMove(SDLKey Key)
{
  unsigned int indexX = m_PlayerPosX;
  unsigned int indexY = m_PlayerPosY;
  unsigned int boxspaceX = indexX;
  unsigned int boxspaceY = indexY;

  switch(Key)
  {
    case SDLK_UP:
    {
      indexY-;
      boxspaceY = indexX - 1;
    }
    break;
    case SDLK_DOWN:
    {
      indexY++;
      boxspaceY = indexX + 1;
    }
    break;
    case SDLK_LEFT:
    {
      indexX-;
      boxspaceX = indexY - 1;
    }
    break;
    case SDLK_RIGHT:
    {
      indexX++;
      boxspaceX = indexY + 1;
    }
    break;
    default:
      break;
  }
  //Check space is floor or destination square
```

```
if((m_CurrentLevel.m_Level[indexX][indexY] ==
  OBJECT_EMPTY) ||
(m_CurrentLevel.m_Level[indexX][indexY] ==
  OBJECT_DEST))
{
  //Check mov array to see if there is a
  //neighbouring box
  if(m_CurrentLevel.MovArray[indexX][indexY] ==
    OBJECT_BOX)
  {
    //If two boxes
    if(m_CurrentLevel.MovArray[boxspaceX]
      [boxspaceY] == OBJECT_BOX)
      return false;

    //If wall
    if(m_CurrentLevel.m_Level[boxspaceX]
      [boxspaceY] == OBJECT_WALL)
      return false;

    //Valid move update
    m_CurrentLevel.MovArray[indexX][indexY] =
      OBJECT_EMPTY;
    m_CurrentLevel.MovArray[boxspaceX]
      [boxspaceY] = OBJECT_BOX;
  }
  //Move the player
  setPlayerPos(indexX, indexY);
}

return false;
}
```

Summary

This chapter completes the game. At this point, Sokoban is playable with the two levels from the design, and, given the level design and tile layout, it's easy to add more. Our game is not without room for improvements, not least the limited number of levels. Better graphics could be added, more animations, and perhaps power ups and game variants. It might also be interesting to add a move counter where some levels must be completed in a specified number of moves.

07

web games

In this chapter you will learn about:

- Flash and Director
- cast members
- sprites
- the Stage
- scripting with JavaScript
- the projector

Computers are incredibly fast, accurate and stupid.
Human beings are incredibly slow, inaccurate and
brilliant. Together they are powerful beyond imagination.

Albert Einstein

7.1 Director

Web games refer to the kind of games people play in web pages. Typically, they are embedded in the HTML page and your browser requires a plug-in to play them. They are usually one of two types, and this reflects the two main plug-ins commonly available: Flash and Shockwave; with Flash being the more common of the two. Both of these are players and are not used to make the actual games. To make them, separate commercial applications are available. To make Flash presentations you need Adobe Flash, and for Shockwave you need Adobe Director (formerly Macromedia Director). This chapter concentrates on Adobe Director, and the reason for this will be explained later.

Both Flash and Director were designed to be multimedia authoring tools. They are easy-to-use packages with drag and drop interfaces. They can make games, interactive displays, DVD shows and so on. Flash is designed to make light web presentations, such as animated websites or movies like those on YouTube.com. It is well suited to this purpose because the player is quick and easy to download, and loads presentations quickly. Director requires the Shockwave player, which is larger to download and loads presentations more slowly, but is better suited to larger, more complex applications like games and 3D software. With Director, presentations can be embedded in web pages, and can also be compiled to a Windows or Mac program. For a long time Director was left at version 2004. By 2007, many people felt it was a dead application and wasn't going to be upgraded. But Adobe have since announced a new version and intend it to play a strong role in the future of web games.

Downloading Director

Director is a commercial application and for long-term use you need to buy a copy. However, a free 30-day trial version can be downloaded from Adobe's site (**http://www.adobe.com**), which will give you the chance to explore it and see if you like it.

Downloading Shockwave

Shockwave is the player for running Director presentations in a browser, and is freely available to download. It is not required for Director presentations that are compiled to executable files. Shockwave can also be installed from Adobe's site.

7.2 Getting started with Director

Director has a comprehensive environment, similar in many ways to Code::Blocks and Visual Studio, but designed to offer a simpler and faster way for creating games and multimedia software. It doesn't offer the complete feature set of fast-paced hardware accelerated graphics, but it is a good solution for 2D games and light 3D games. In the next chapter, Director will be used to create a game of Hex.

Hex is a simple board game to play, but it will also sport a basic AI (Artificial Intelligence) that can think and compete against the player.

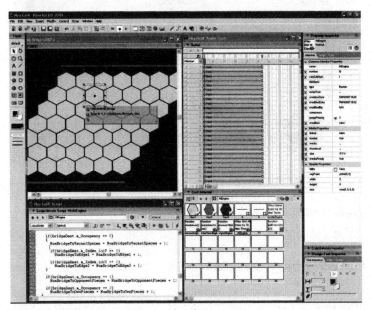

Figure 7.1 The Director window

The stage

The stage is a window of the final presentation. It contains an inner and an outer rectangle. Anything inside the rectangle is on stage, and anything outside is off stage. When someone plays your game, they will only see what is on stage. Obviously, events on the stage can change and will be animated over time so the status of the stage can change, and objects can move on and off stage as required.

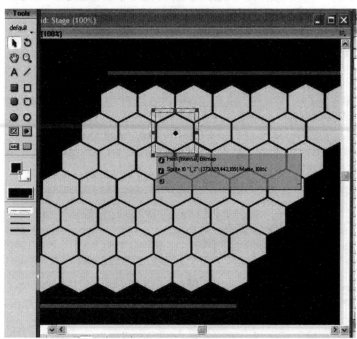

Figure 7.2 The Stage

The cast

As in a movie, the cast represents all the things that will feature in your game – all the objects that can appear on stage. These can be graphics loaded from files, sounds, video, and even other Director presentations. The cast is a list of all the resources a game will use. Each one will have a name and unique identifier, which Director will use to reference each cast member.

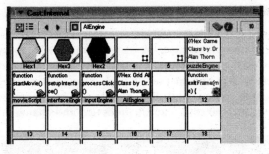

Figure 7.3 The Cast window

Sprites

The relationship between the cast and the sprites is like that between classes and instances. A cast member may be a bitmap loaded from a file, but what appears on the stage is a sprite. It is an instance of that cast member. If I wanted two copies of an image on the stage, I would have two sprites which are associated with the same cast member. This way, no duplicate resources are loaded into memory.

Time line

The window represents the flow of the game, and the progress of time from frame to frame. Sprites appear here as long grey blocks, spanning the frames in which they appear. It's possible to jump playback to specific frames, or to loop between two frames, and so on – playback is not necessarily linear. The grey block represents a sprite on the stage and its length shows its lifetime on stage. If the time line enters a frame beyond a grey block, then that sprite will not be on stage at that frame.

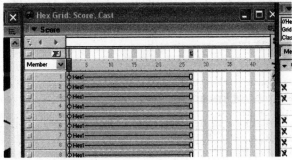

Figure 7.4 The Time line window

Scripting

The Scripting window is where you do the programming. Director can use two languages; its own proprietary language, Lingo, and JavaScript. This book will use JavaScript as it's similar to C++ and widely documented. Using scripting, almost all aspects of the game can be controlled. Sprites and cast members can be adjusted, and the stage can be processed and changed.

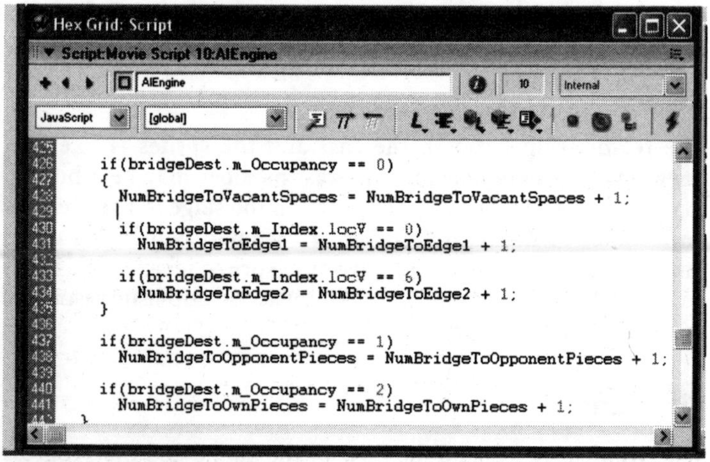
Hex Grid: Script
Script:Movie Script 10:AIEngine
AIEngine
10
Internal
JavaScript
[global]
if(bridgeDest.m_Occupancy == 0)
{
NumBridgeToVacantSpaces = NumBridgeToVacantSpaces + 1;
if(bridgeDest.m_Index.locV == 0)
NumBridgeToEdge1 = NumBridgeToEdge1 + 1;
if(bridgeDest.m_Index.locV == 6)
NumBridgeToEdge2 = NumBridgeToEdge2 + 1;
}
if(bridgeDest.m_Occupancy == 1)
NumBridgeToOpponentPieces = NumBridgeToOpponentPieces + 1;
if(bridgeDest.m_Occupancy == 2)
NumBridgeToOwnPieces = NumBridgeToOwnPieces + 1;

Figure 7.5 The Scripting window

7.3 Cast members

Director cast members are resources. They are imported media files, including background images, sprites, text, sound, music and anything else featured in the game. All the cast members are stored in a list in the Cast Member Window. From here, they can be sorted, arranged and given names and IDs. By default each cast member has a unique number; starting from 1. These identifications are important because in scripting, the numbers will be used to identify cast members.

Adding cast members

A cast member can be any of the following types: BMP, JPEG, PNG, TGA, PICT, SOUND (.WAV, .MP3), AVI, Flash, Shockwave, RealMedia, Quick Time and animated GIF.

To add a cast member to a project:

1 Select **File > Import**.

2 Select a file.

3 There will be a drop-down box labelled **Media**, where you can choose *Standard Import* or *Link to External File*. *Standard Import* will load the entire file into the project, so that it can run independently without the file being present. *Link to External File* requires it to be distributed with the project. This option is good if the file may need to be replaced or changed after the project is compiled.

4 Click **OK**.

Editing cast member properties

Each cast member can be thought of as a class, and like most classes, they have properties. A cast member will have at least a name and an ID; if it's an image it will also have width and height properties. To change the properties, the Property Inspector window can be used. They can also be changed at run time using JavaScript, and this is considered later.

Adding cast members to the stage as sprites

Cast members can be added to the stage by dragging their icon onto it from the Cast Member window. They can also be added by dragging them onto the time line. Once on the stage, an instance is created and this is called a sprite. Sprites have a lifespan in the time line.

7.4   Sprites and the stage

The stage is the visual area of the game. It represents what the player will see. Sprites are the actors on stage. The time line window shows and controls the flow of a game. If you press the **Play** icon on the toolbar (or click **Control > Play**), the game is run. This is similar to running an application in Code::Blocks or Visual C++. As playback begins, a slider runs across the top of the time line until it reaches the end, when the game stops. The slider acts as a marker for the current moment in the game. Whatever sprites exist beneath it at the time will appear on stage.

Managing sprites

Sprites are like classes, and have properties, which can be edited using the property inspector. Sprites have names, numbers, width and height and positions on stage in terms of pixels (x,y). Many sprites of types can also be transformed – scaled and/or rotated.

Some of the important sprite properties are considered below. Most of these can be changed using the Property Inspector.

◆ *locH* and *locV* – define the (x,y) position on stage. They are also refered to as X and Y, but in JavaScript, use these terms.

◆ *W* and *H* – stand for width and height. These properties can be changed for image-based sprites (not sound, etc.). The sprite will be scaled to the specified size.

◆ *Member* – the name of the cast member associated with the sprite. It can be changed; even at runtime. For example, two frames of an animation could be loaded in as 'Member1' and 'Member2'. There may be only one sprite, but its *Member* property could be changed to animate between the frames.

◆ *SpriteNum* – the unique number of the sprite, which can be used to identify the sprite in JavaScript.

◆ *Name* – a human-readable name. It can be used to identify a sprite in JavaScript if the names are unique.

7.5 Sprites and the time line

Anything on the stage is considered a sprite and becomes part of the time line. This defines all the events that happen from the beginning to the end of a game. When Play is pressed, the presentation begins. The slider scrolls from to left to right, frame by frame until it reaches the end and stops. Each cell on the time line is considered one frame. The numbers on the time line header label the frames, usually in increments of 5. All of this can be examined in the Time Line window.

Channels

Each row in the Time Line window is called a *channel*. Each channel has a number and these are marked in the left-hand margin, beginning at 1. The sprites on the stage will appear in the time line, as extended blue blocks. You can use the mouse to drag them around, and you can adjust the length of the blocks to change the length of time they appear on stage. Each sprite occupies a different channel in the time line and no two sprites can occupy the same one simultaneously. The channels determine the Z order of sprites on stage – which sprites are in front of others, with sprites in Channel 1 at the back of the stage. (See page 84 for more on the Z order.)

- You can drag sprites into different channels to change their Z order.

Sprites, animation and key frames

Much of the animation for games will be achieved through scripting. However, rigging up some animations in Director can be done very quickly just by pointing and clicking. Animation like this can be achieved by 'key framing'.

Key frames

Key frames are the important, defining moments of an animation. For example, let's take a boy raising his arm to scratch his head, in a total set of 100 frames. The animation begins at frame 0 (arms by his side). As it progresses, frame by frame, the arm will gradually raise to scratch his head by frame 100. During the course of the animation we may note a number of crucial parts. By frame 25, his arm will be bent, perhaps a quarter of the way in the air. By 50, the arm will be closer to the head and the hand posed like a claw, ready to scratch, and so on. These defining moments are key frames. Using Director, you can specify the positions of sprites at key moments in an animation, and Director will fill in all the intervening frames for you.

To create a set of key frames:

1 Right-click on a sprite in the time line.

2 Select **Edit Sprite Frames**. This opens up the sprite block to show each of the frames from which it is composed.

3 Select a frame in the sprite block and then adjust the sprite in stage. For example, move it to one side.

4 Go back to the time line and choose a different frame in the sprite block, several frames away from the previous key frame.

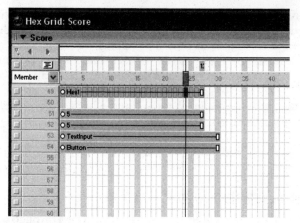

Figure 7.6 Creating key frames

Move the sprite again, to the other side of the stage.

5   To close the block, right-click on the sprite and select **Edit Entire Sprite**.

6   Now press Play to see the results and watch the sprite move. Notice how Director fills in the intervening frames.

Selecting the sprite on stage shows its animation path. This is the route the sprite will take when play is pressed. You can adjust the route by holding down the **[Alt]** key. With **[Alt]** held down, click and drag the path points.

7.6   Getting started with scripting

When the Play button is pressed, the presentation begins. It will normally stop when the slider reaches the end of the time line. However, most games don't work like that, but continue through the game loop until the user decides to exit. Creating this kind of behaviour introduces us to scripting.

Scripting with JavaScript

With scripting, almost every aspect of Director can be automated. Sprites can be changed, the time line can be edited, and user input can be processed. Director offers two scripting languages to choose from, Lingo or JavaScript. We will choose JavaScript because it's similar to C++ and easy to use. Some knowledge of JavaScript is assumed.

Script types

A Director project may have many scripts. Each script is like a source file, and it can contain functions, events, objects, and so on. If a player clicks a button, a script needs to define what happens. As a movie begins, a script can be called to perform initial processing, and so on. There a several types of scripts:

Sprite behaviour script

These are attached to sprites on the stage, and are handlers for events that apply to the sprite, such as mouse clicks, and movement. A sprite may have many different scripts attached to it.

Movie scripts

These are global scripts attached to the movie as a whole. They can handle all kinds of events, from user input, to frame changes. For games, these kinds of scripts are vital.

Frame scripts

These are attached to a frame and can be called as it begins or ends. This kind of script will be used to prevent the final frame from ending automatically, so the game continues until the player decides to exit.

The Script window

Once a script is created it becomes part of the cast like any other object. Scripts are edited using the Script window. This can be opened by adding a new frame script, or it can be opened manually by clicking the Script window icon, or by using the menu commands **Window > Script**.

The Edit box lets you assign the script a name, and the Property Inspector can be used to change its properties. For example, you can change its status from a behaviour to a movie script, and so on. The window can also be used to select the language – though a script can only be in one language, not a mixture of both.

Creating a frame script

The first script to create will be a frame script to stop the presentation ending. Consider the following.

1   In the Time Line window, double-click in the cell above the last frame. This cell appears above the frame number bar.

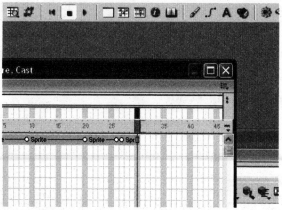

Figure 7.7 Select the last frame

2   A Script window will appear and invite you to edit the frame handler. You will see the following text.

```
function exitFrame(me)
{
}
```

•   The code may initially appear in Lingo instead of JavaScript. To change this, select **JavaScript** from the drop-down list at the top of the Script window.

3   Add the following code to the Script.

```
function exitFrame(me)
{
    movie.go(_movie.frame);
}
```

4   Run the presentation. Now the time slider stops at the last frame and doesn't exit until the Stop button is pressed. The example code uses the *movie* class to keep looping at the current frame each time **exitFrame** is called. This event is called each time the frame ends.

7.7 Scripting objects and events

Movie scripts apply globally across the presentation and can be used to access any of the stage sprites, cast members and the time line. They can process user input and handle events.

To create a movie script:

1 Open the Script window. Click the Script Window icon or click **Window > Script**.

2 The script should automatically be set to a movie script. This setting can be changed by using the Property Inspector.

3 In the Property Inspector, click the **Script** tab and use the drop-down list to set the script type. This should now have created a blank movie script ready to use.

Handling events

Events can be triggered by all kinds of things, such as a mouse click, a key press, every change of frame, the start or the end of a movie, and so on. In Director, events can be handled in script. Director associates every event with a named function. When the event occurs, it searches the movie scripts to see if an appropriate function has been implemented. If it has, the function is called. If no function exists, the event is ignored or the default handling takes over. For example, on a mouse click, Director searches for **mouseDown** function. If one has been defined to handle clicks, then it is called.

These functions handle some common events:

◆ **startMovie** – called when a movie begins, before the first frame.

◆ **StepFrame** – called when a move enters a new frame.

◆ **mouseDown, mouseUp** – called when the mouse button is pressed and released.

◆ **keyDown, keyUp** – called when keys are pressed and released.

Sample code

```
function keyDown(me)
  {
    _player.alert("You pressed a key");
  }
```

> The above functions are special because they are attached to events, but you are not limited to them. You can create as many as needed, and name them as you please.

7.8 Core classes

To program Director effectively it's important to know the core classes as you must deal with these objects frequently. They include classes for the movie, the sprites on stage and the cast members. Using these classes it's possible to control a presentation completely. The following subsections look briefly at each class. For a full list of the methods and properties, please consult the Director documentation.

Movie and Player class

Together the Movie and Player classes help you control the Director movie. The Movie class is an overall manager, and the Player class includes methods to quit and pause the movie. It also features methods to show messages boxes on the screen.

Movie class methods:

* **go** – jumps to the specified frame.
* **delay** – pauses the movie for a specified time.

Movie class properties:

* **path** – path of the current movie file.
* **frame** – the current frame.

Player class methods:

* **alert** – shows a message on screen.
* **quit** – exits.

Sample code

```
//Go to frame 5
  _movie.go(5);

//Say hello
  _player.alert("hello");
```

Sprite class

The Sprite class encapsulates a sprite on the stage. It can be used to transform sprites, move or animate them and so on. The **Sprite** function will return the sprite for a given number.

Sprite class properties:

- **blend** – value between 0 and 100 that specifies transparency, where 0 = invisible and 100 = opaque.
- **locV, locH** – (x, y) position.
- **member** – pointer to the cast member associated with the sprite.
- **rect** – the rectangular region of the sprite.
- **rotation** – the angle of rotation of the sprite.

Sample code

```
//Get sprite 1
  var mySprite = sprite(1);

  mySprite.blend = 100; //Make it visible

//Set sprite position
  mySprite.locH = 300;
  mySprite.locV = 700;
```

Mouse class

The Mouse class is used on input events to determine the cursor position and button properties.

Mouse class properties:

- **mouseDown** – TRUE or FALSE.
- **mouseLoc** – point structure for cursor X and Y.

Sample code

```
//Determines if mouse click was on sprite
function mouseUp()
{
  var mySprite = sprite(1);
```

```
if(_mouse.mouseLoc.inside(mySprite.rect)==true)
{
    _player.alert("mouse is inside");
}
}
```

7.8 Publishing with the Projector

In Director, presentations are compiled using the Projector. In compilation, the presentation is collated, verified and then packaged as either a Windows or Mac program, or as a web game. Web games are played via a browser, embedded in web pages.

Before running the Projector, adjust its settings to your needs:

1 Use **File > Publish Settings** to open the **Settings** window.

2 Specify the compilation type – Windows, Mac, web game, etc. You can also have Director generate a web page for you, with the presentation already embedded. This screen allows you to adjust the settings for the web page.

3 Click **OK**.

To compile a project:

1 Click **File > Publish**.

2 It may ask you to save the project before compiling.

3 Once compiled the presentation will be generated. If it is an executable program, an exe file will be created in the project directory. If it was a web project, an appropriate presentation file and web page will be generated. The Shockwave plug-in is required to play the presentation.

Summary

This chapter has explored Adobe Director. It explained how to create presentations and build them using the projector. Additionally, it considered the concepts of the stage, the cast, sprites, the time line and scripting. Scripting especially, is important for web games made in Director, because scripts are crucial for customizing behaviour.

08

artificial
intelligence

In this chapter you will learn:

- how to program artificial
  intelligence
- about path finding
- about finite state machines
- about heuristic algorithms
- about state-driven behaviour

The question of whether machines can think is about as relevant as the question of whether submarines can swim.

Edsger Dijkstra

8.1 What is AI?

Artificial Intelligence (AI) is a broad field of study. In the context of computer games, AI is what makes a game think for itself in response to the player, or at least *appear* to think. So long as the computer can take appropriate actions within the context of the game, and so long as it remains believable to the gamer, then AI for games serves its purpose. In some games, for example, chess, the AI can be so good that the computer can beat all but the best human players. AI is not limited to deciding how the computer acts in two-player turn-based games, but is also used to simulate other kinds of intelligence. For example, a tactical ops game might feature a squadron of elite soldiers who need to negotiate a dangerous hostage situation. In such circumstances the player can issue commands to different officers and other subordinates, commands like 'Cover me' or 'Search and destroy'. Once a command is issued, the computer characters, called NPCs (non-player character), will run off and follow orders. The player doesn't need to tell the NPCs where to walk or how to get to their destinations, and nor do they need to tell the computer who are enemies and who are not. The NPCs work this out for themselves through AI.

8.2 Intelligent Hex

To explore some of the fundamental concepts underpinning AI, this chapter examines how to make a game of Hex, in which the computer will be able to think about its moves and pose a basic challenge to the player. Hex is a two-player turn-based game set on a hexagonal grid. This should be equal in width and height, and though there are no formal restrictions placed on the size of the board, we will use a 7×7 board.

The rules of hex

1 There are two players, blue (player) and red (AI). Each player takes turns, and blue has the first move.

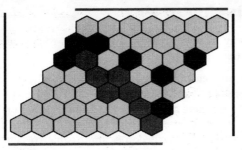

Figure 8.1 A Hex grid

2 The game begins with each hexagon in the grid being empty. (We will be referring to hexagons as 'cells'.)

3 On each turn a player puts down a single coloured piece into any empty cell on the board. The objective is to build a connected path of your pieces, linking the opposite sides of the board which match your colour. Your opponent attempts to do the same.

4 The winner is the player who connects their opposite sides first.

About Hex

Hex was independently invented by Piet Henn in 1942 and John Nash in 1947. Since then it has provided endless fascination among strategists and gamers alike. Many attempts have been made to 'solve' Hex, which means people have used computers to find good responses to each move. The ultimate aim is to create a combination of moves that always leads to a winning solution. Though it is agreed the first player has a significant advantage in this game, it's quite easy to lose that advantage unless you play an exact combination of moves. Naturally, the larger the board, the more complex the game becomes, and for this reason, many larger size versions of Hex remain unsolved.

Play Hex!

Before going any further, it might be helpful to play a game of Hex. There are lots of free Hex games online, for two players and to play against AI.

8.3   The joy of Hex

The best way to start creating a Hex AI is to consider some of the properties of the game.

+ **Hex cannot end in a draw.** This has mathematically been proven to be so, and looking at the board it's easy to see how. Not only are there a finite number of moves, but once a player makes a single connected path to their opposing sides of the board it immediately becomes impossible for the opponent to do the same.

+ **The first player has the advantage** and like most games of this kind, the ideal starting move is to the centre cell. Because of this, there are variations of Hex where the starting player is forbidden from choosing this opening. We will adopt this rule because it makes the game more interesting.

+ **The centre area of the board is the most important place** because from here a player can form many paths to their edges. This means the player who controls the centre of the board is likely to be the winner, though not always.

Let's consider some of the basic moves available in Hex. At first sight, a player might be tempted to put their pieces down in a line, or from side to side, each one resting beside the previous. This is likely to end up as a losing strategy as it's easy for the opponent to block; or even worse, your opponent may let you pursue this dangerous course, wasting moves until you almost reach the end and then set-up a blockade. To win a serious game of Hex there are a series of more subtle formations that players adopt. To make a Hex AI, it's important to understand these.

Two-way bridge

One of the most fundamental strategies in Hex is the bridge. It is where two non-adjacent pieces, say x and y, have two empty

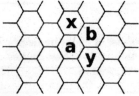

Figure 8.2 A two-way bridge

neighbouring cells, a and b, in common. This is a useful way of assuring connections. If the red player occupies x and y, and both a and b are empty, red must be able to bridge the gap. If blue moves to cell a, red can respond by moving to b, and vice versa.

From the perspective of the Red Player who occupies both x and y, the bridge can be categorized as being in one of three states.

* **Open** – where both a and b are empty.

* **Threatened** – where one cell, a or b, is empty and the other is occupied by the opponent. Red can save this connection by moving to the empty space, or risk losing the bridge if they move elsewhere.

* **Closed** – where both cells are occupied, either by one player entirely or between both.

Blocks

This could be a variety of moves and there is no standard formation, but the idea is that by moving to one cell it will block the route of the opponent, either directly or via bridging. Determining whether a move will block an opponent as well as serve your interests can be a deciding factor when faced with a choice of moves.

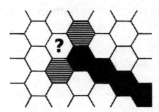

Figure 8.3 Blocking a line

Centre moves

The first moves generally occur in the centre of the board for good reason – they lead to the maximum number of connections that can be made while also blocking the opponent. It is also ideal if, given the choice, moves can remain as close to the centre as possible, leaving room for manoeuvre in either direction.

8.4   The making of Hex

```
function hexCell(x, y)
{
  this.m_Index = point(x, y);
  //Location on board e.g. (0,3)
  this.m_Occupancy = 0;
  //0 = vacant, 1=player, 2=AI

  this.m_Adjacency = new Array();
  //Array of adjacent cells
  this.m_Bridges = new Array();
  //Any bridges to other cells
}
```

Remember, in JavaScript classes are declared like functions, and member properties are prefixed by *this*.

One of the simplest ways to program a Hex grid is to create two classes, one for a hex cell and one for the overall grid that will be a collection of cells, as shown above. The grid will arrange the cells in a two-dimensional array where the top left cell is (0,0) and the bottom right cell is (6,6). Any Hex cell on the board can be in only one of three states; 0 = vacant, 1 = occupied by a blue piece (the player) or 2 = occupied by a red piece. The winning condition for blue is to have an unbroken chain of blue pieces reaching from top to bottom, and the aim for red is a chain of red pieces from left to right.

Notice how each cell maintains a list of pointers to its connecting cells. This isn't absolutely necessary but it makes processing and reasoning about the board easier and quicker for the AI. Notice also how each cell keeps a list of bridges, i.e. a list of all cells which have a bridge connection to this cell.

Usually when a person plays Hex they have a strategy in mind. They may aim to make their first move in the centre (3,3), or nearby, then afterwards build two-way bridges outwards from the centre so a connection from each opposing side can easily be made. So a player begins with an initial aggressive strategy that aims at connecting their sides, but the response of the opponent will also cause them to make changes in their own plans. They may change to an alternative aggressive strategy because the opponent might block their path. On the other hand, especially dangerous moves from an opponent will cause players to adopt defensive positions. This kind of decision-making process by AI is called *state-driven behaviour*. That is, the AI may resolve to start aggressively (initial state) and then circumstances may cause it to change defensively (new state). The actual mechanics that define how state-driven behaviour works is known as a **Finite State Machine (FSM)**.

NOTE. Traffic lights are one of the simplest forms of FSMs. Finite state machines are a behavioural model composed of various states, and often these states have corresponding actions. For example, the traffic light is red. That is its current state, and it means stop. After it has been red long enough, the state needs to change to another state; so an action is taken. The lights change and the state becomes amber. Again, after a short time, the state needs to change again and so an action changes the light to a new state, green. Later it will return to red and the whole process repeats again.

For a game of Hex then, AI can assume one of the several potential states on each move. Naturally, depending on the state of the board and order of play, the AI will change from one state to another; though the initial state will be aggressive. The following is a list of states the AI can assume.

1 **Bridge building** – in this state the AI will look at ways of making two-way bridges, hopefully to connect its sides of the board. On any turn there might be a long list of bridges the computer can make. We will look later at how the AI can decide which bridge is best, and why some bridges are better to make than others.

2 **Connecting edges** – this state will make the AI play a move aimed at connecting its existing bridges, and will favour moves based on whether it also blocks or obstructs the opponent.

3 **Forced moves** – when the AI can win; or when the player is one move away from winning, and it's possible to block them. Forced moves are ones that simply must be played. Another situation is when the player threatens one of the AI's two-way bridges by putting a piece into one of the two connecting cells that join an AI's bridge. If the AI doesn't move to the other cell this turn, then it risks losing the bridge because the player can occupy the second connecting cell on the next turn and break the overall bridge connection.

♦ Naturally, the AI can be improved or refined by adding more states.

The effects of the Finite State Machine will become apparent later. Let's first take a look at how the AI handles the opening moves.

8.5 Opening moves – game trees

In our game of Hex, the human player moves first. As the centre cell (3,3) is disabled, the player can choose from 48 different starting cells, with some being a better choice than others. The player may be likely to pick (3,4) or (4,3), or some similar cell that connects to the centre, but such a move cannot be guaranteed even though it's probable.

Once the player has moved, how should the AI respond? The first thing it should aim to do is build bridges because that's the easiest way to establish connections across the board, but it also needs to take account of the player's strategy which cannot be judged from just the first move. Therefore, to handle this first response, the Hex AI will use a *game tree*. It is a list of moves and responses, but structured like a tree. Its leaves, or nodes, are all different permutations that can arise and the AI response to them. It is a pre-planned AI that doesn't use real-time calculations, searching and processing – it's a look-up architecture. The player makes their opening move and the AI scans the game tree

Move 1

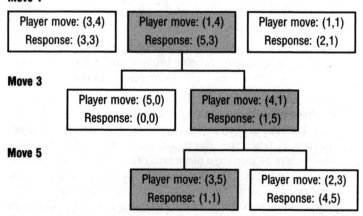

Figure 8.4 Opening moves in Hex

until it finds a node which matches the move, and this will also contain the AI's response. Some simple AI games are entirely based on game trees, but because of all the possible combinations on our 7×7 Hex board, a tree isn't feasible or fun for the whole game's AI, so it will be used for the first move only. It could be expanded for later moves; but would handle only the most common combinations, rather than every possible move.

Programming the tree

The following functions create the game tree and search it. Only one move and response node has been written into the create function – you will need to add more nodes to the same pattern.

Create game tree:

```
function treeNode()
{
  this.playerMove = point(0,0);
  //If player moves here
  this.aiResponse = point(0,0);
  //Then AI Moves here
}

function createTree()
{
  this.m_Nodes = new Array();
  //Tree nodes storing moves
  var openingMove1 = new treeNode();
  openingMove1.PlayerMove = point(3,4);
  openingMove1.AiResponse = point(4,5);
  this.m_Nodes.push(openingMove1);
  //Add more moves
}
```

Search game tree:

```
//Argument PlayerMove = move this turn, eg (3,2)
function checkTree(PlayerMove)
{
  //Check tree for player move, then respond

  for(var i =0; i< this.m_Nodes.length; i++)
```

```
{
    if(this.m_Nodes[i].PlayerMove == PlayerMove)
        return this.m_Nodes[i]. AiResponse;
}
return NULL;
}
```

> The JavaScript code for the Hex AI is in the (.DIR) file. This
> is a Director project file. It can be opened and run using
> Adobe Director. A free trial version of Director can be
> downloaded from http://www.adobe.com/products/director/

8.6 Moves – heuristic algorithms

After the opening moves from the game tree, the AI will make
future moves reflecting its state according to the FSM. Some
facts, however, can be established here:

- The computer needs to take account of cells currently occupied
  by the player and AI, as it is not possible to move to them, so
  the number of potential cells to consider can be reduced.

- With the exception of danger moves, which we will return to
  shortly, the AI will only consider adjacent squares, or those
  that can be bridged to, from any of its current pieces. As the
  board ends up becoming more populated, this list of potential
  squares can become quite numerous, but it's a good
  mechanism to narrow the search, and good for guiding the
  AI in the right direction towards a useful strategy.

Now the number of cells the AI can move to in any turn has
been reduced, these should be examined in more detail.

- Bridge-building means the AI goes searching about the board
  for available bridges to make, but it's likely to find many
  bridges so how does it decide which one is best?

- The forced-move state indicates the AI must play a defensive
  move, but which one should it be? And how does it know
  when it needs to play such a move anyway?

- If the AI enters a connecting-edge state, which move is the best for connecting bridges and edges, and how does the AI determine when to stop building bridges and when to start connecting them?

Forced moves

After the opening move, the first course of action the AI should consider on every turn is whether to play a forced move – either the AI must play one now, or it must not. Forced moves are brought about when either the player or the computer is one move away from winning, and the AI must either block the player if possible, or play the winning move. (Section 8.7 explains how winning states can be detected using path finding.)

A forced move can also be caused when an AI bridge comes under threat by the player. If the player has occupied one of the connecting cells between a bridge, the AI would normally want to occupy the remaining cell and complete the bridge, though there may be some circumstances when a more advanced AI will want to avoid protecting a bridge and to play a different move instead. Bridges are such an easy way to connect edges, and in most cases this will be the correct move to play. Let's take a look a some sample code to determine a broken bridge.

```
//Class to represent a bridge on the board.
//A board will contain an array of bridge
//structures representing each bridge.
//On each turn the bridges will be updated
//reflecting the current state of the board.
//e.g. the status - whether it is open, etc.

function bridge()
{
   this.SourceCell;
   //Pointer to Source of the bridge
   this.DestCell;
   //Pointer to Dest of the bridge
   this.ConnectionCell1;
   //Pointer to Intervening Cell 1
   this.ConnectionCell2;
   //Pointer to Intervening Cell 2
```

```
  this.Status = 0;
  // 0 = Open 1=Threatened 2=Closed
}

function checkBrokenBridges()
{
  for(var i =0; i<this.Bridges.count; i++)
  {
    if(this.Bridges[i].Status != 1)
      continue;
    //If bridge source and dest are AI
    if((this.Bridges[i].SourceCell.m_Occupancy==2)
      && (this.Bridges[i].DestCell.m_Occupancy==2))
    {
      if((this.Bridges[i].ConnectionCell1.
        m_Occupancy==1)||(this.Bridges[i].
          ConnectionCell2.m_Occupancy==1))
      {
        //Threatened by player
        //Rate connection as being high priority
        //to move this turn and return

        rateCell(ConnectionCell1);
        return ConnectionCell1;
      }
    }
  }
  return NULL;
}
```

Bridge building

The bridge-building state of the FSM makes the AI play a move
that creates a two-way bridge to at least one existing AI piece
already on the board. The purpose is to create enough bridge
connections so the opposing sides can be connected. The bridge-
building state will have top priority after a forced-move state.
Before building a bridge, however, the AI should ensure it is
necessary. After all, enough bridges might already have been built
to create a winning connection. If this is true, bridge building
should stop and the FSM state changes to edge-connecting, which

is the lowest priority state. The job of the Bridge Building function is not simply to pick any cell that is a bridge, but also to decide which cell leads to the best bridge at this point in the game. The function given below rates all the potential bridges and decides which is the best. This kind of function is called a *heuristic algorithm* because its intention is to generate a cost or score, and suggests to us which choice is best or which way is the right way to go. In this case, which bridge shall we make?

Technically, each cell on the board can have up to six bridge connections to some other cell on the board. So if we were given a board after three turns have been played, there will be three existing AI pieces and so we would have up to 18 bridge connections to consider for this turn. Of course, some of the existing pieces might be on the edge, and some might bridge to duplicate cells or occupied ones, so the real number of cells to examine would usually be less than this. It's important to remember we're only interested in unoccupied cells that we can move to. The idea is to cycle through all of them and to rate each one based on how valuable it is to move to. Each of these cells is then popped on a list and arranged according to their score. The highest scoring cell is the one to move to. The following source code demonstrates how a cell is rated.

```
//Scoring System
var BridgeToOwnPiece = 1;
var BridgeToOpponent = 2;
var BridgeToEmpty = 1;
var BridgeToEdge = 2;


//Argument of function will be any vacant cell
//that bridges from any cell already occupied by
//the player. So, given a cell this function
//rates its desirability as a bridge.

function rateBridge(currentCell)
{
  //Get a list of all bridges from this cell,
  //i.e all where this cell is a source or Dest

  var bridgeList = getBridges(); //An array

  //Count the number of times a bridge may be an
```

```
//opponent, an empty space, an edge etc.
var BridgeOwnCount = 0;
var BridgeEdgeCount = 0;
var BridgeOpponentCount = 0;
var BridgeEmptyCount = 0;

//Cycle through attaching bridges
for(var i = 0; i < bridgeList.length; i++)
{
  if(bridgeOpponent()==true)
  {
    BridgeOpponentCount=BridgeOpponentCount+1;
    continue;
  }
//...And so on, score for each position
}
```

```
//Compute score
var BridgeOpponentScore = BridgeOpponentCount
  * BridgeToOpponent;

var BridgeOwnScore = BridgeOwnCount *
  BridgeToOwnPiece;

var BridgeEmptyScore = BridgeEmptyCount *
  BridgeToEmpty;

var BridgeEdgeCount = BridgeEdgeCount *
  BridgeToEdge;

var TotalScore = BridgeOpponentScore +
  BridgeOwnScore + BridgeEmptyScore +
  BridgeEdgeCount;
return TotalScore;
}
```

Edge-connection

Having found no forced move to process and having exhausted all bridge options, the AI is in an edge-connection state. The AI will implicitly know when to cease bridge building and to begin connecting. It will determine this either because there are no open bridges left to be built, or because given the current set of bridges belonging to the AI it would be possible to generate a winning connection by joining the bridges. (The next section explains how winning connections can be determined.) In edge-connection mode, the AI will attempt to connect any open bridges which it owns and attempt to forge connections to the edges. The order and exact positioning of these new connections will be subject to a heuristic algorithm. Each potential cell that can be moved to will be rated to determine which cell is the best on any current turn. It will be rated according to how many same colour cells it neighbours, whether it's on the edge, whether it interrupts the opponent's connection, and so on.

8.7 Winning states

Obviously the objective for the AI is to win the game by connecting its opposing sides of the board, and the player will be trying to do the same. Therefore, the AI should have a way of asking 'If I move here can I win the game?' or 'If the player moves there will I lose the game?'. If the answer to either of those questions is 'Yes', then the AI will need to make a forced move, either to win the game or to block their opponent. As a result then, the AI needs to determine when a win has occurred and also if a win will be likely to occur as a result of a move.

Look at the Hex grid diagram on page 111. How is it possible to determine when a winning connection is made? To the human eye it is simple to see because we can simply trace our finger along the connection and if it touches both sides in an unbroken chain then a win has occurred. But the AI must think in terms of the Hex grid, in terms of references such as (3,3) and (4,5), and whether or not those cells are occupied. An initial approach might be to run along a single row or column and to test whether every cell is occupied by the same player. If so, it would indeed mean a win for that player, but in most games connections are not made as a long unbroken chain in a single row or column. Often the connections are winding and snake-like. Inevitably, an important condition for a win will be to test whether a player has at least one of their pieces in each of their opposing sides. This is because these mark where the connections begin and end. But this in itself cannot be taken as a win because those edge pieces may not be linked by intervening pieces across the board.

Path finding

The solution to this process is path finding. Essentially, this is about finding a route from one destination to another, from x to y. Often computers will be seeking the shortest path between two points, but it can be used to find all kinds of paths. In this case, the intention is to find a path from any cell on one side to any cell on the opposing side so long as all cells in the connection are of the same colour, red or blue.

Path finding has a wide application in the gaming world. Imagine an FPS game, where an axe-wielding maniac of an NPC has decided to attack the player using a close range weapon. The NPC has spotted the player in the distance, from the window of a room several blocks away. It would look unbelievable if the NPC generated a direct path to the player and followed this unbroken line through walls, over water and past any obstacles as though none of them were really there. If the player is subject to the laws of physics and cannot pass through solid objects then why should NPCs be able to? Instead, the computer should navigate their way through the world like the player has to. To reach the player the NPC must walk down stairs, travel through doorways and not walls, and they should avoid obstacles, and use only valid, sensible paths. Path finding does this by splitting up the game world into a graph, putting important nodes at specific points so all of them are joined by straight lines. Using a number of path-finding algorithms like *Dijkstra's Algorithm* and *A** (pronounced A-Star), the route between two points can be found. This chapter examines the beginnings of Dijkstra's Algorithm for the purposes of Hex.

Finding the connection using islands

We must start by looking at the concept of *islands*. An island is a cluster of connected cells that are occupied by the same colour. A single cell occupied by, say, blue and which has no adjacent cells of the same colour is considered an island of one, but where there are two or more connected cells of the same colour, these are together considered a single island. Using this concept, a win for any player can be defined as a single island which has at least one piece on each of their opposing edge cells. We know this to be true because if each of the pieces on the opposing edges were not connected then they would not be part of the same island.

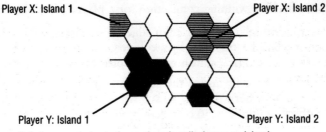

Player X: Island 1
Player X: Island 2
Player Y: Island 1
Player Y: Island 2

Figure 8.4 A connected set of one player's cells forms an island

Implementing islands for path finding

Each island can be represented by an integer. The Hex grid will keep an overall counter of how many islands each player has, and each Hex cell will have an integer property indicating which island it belongs to. This value can be 1 or higher. Each time a move on the board is made, the island number of each cell may be updated, or some of them might remain unchanged depending on whether a move connects up a group of previously unconnected islands. The general algorithm for determining a winning connection is outlined below. Because of its length, the full code is not given here, but it can be found on the online code.

On each move, a piece X is placed on the board:

1 The island counter is incremented. If this is the first move then *island count* will be 1 since only 1 island exists. *island count* is then assigned to piece X as its *island* number. So X is a member of island number 1.

2 Scan all cells adjacent to X. If no adjacent cell is the same colour as X, then no further processing is required and X is a new island on its own; terminate process. If any adjacent cell is occupied by the same colour as X, then X is connected to one or more existing islands. Move to step 3.

3 For every adjacent cell of the same colour as X, find the lowest *island* number among them and assign this to X and to every other adjacent cell of the same colour. Adjacent cells of X may in turn be connected to other adjacent cells of the same colour, making them part of the same island. It is important to cycle recursively through all adjacent cells so that every cell in the island shares the same *island* number.

4 Repeat this process for every move.

So, to test for a winning connection for a player of colour C:

1 Cycle through every cell in an edge column or row (E1). For each cell in E1 occupied by a colour C, find a corresponding cell in Edge 2 (E2) that is also occupied by C.

2 If two edge cells are of the same colour test to see if their *island* numbers match. If so, the edges are connected. Otherwise, there is no connection between them.

8.8 Super Hex

Though this chapter does not consider them in detail, there are a number of ways our game of Hex can be substantially improved. Neural networks, genetic algorithms and fuzzy logic can all be employed to make the AI even tougher. But not just tougher – the AI can be made to learn from mistakes it made in previous games, so that it does not repeat them when faced with similar situations. Of course, with such improvements there comes a price of greater processing demands, and the time taken for the AI to consider their moves is greatly increased. This may not be acceptable for games because players don't expect the computer to take too long calculating its moves.

Neural networks

Neural networks base themselves on the way humans are said to learn things from a neurological perspective, hence the name. Using a neural network allows programmers to make software that learns, within limits. It means if a programmer developed a sufficiently accomplished neural network, they could then design a reasonably stupid hex AI that learned more each time it played. To begin with, the AI might not be impressive, but on each subsequent game, it would become progressively more difficult to defeat. It might never reach the standard of unbeatable, especially if it plays as the second player (see page 112), but it can become a formidable opponent.

Genetic algorithms

Another form of AI was inspired by genetics and evolution. *Genetic algorithms* tend not to be used for creating AI opponents in games, but are employed to find solutions to complex problems. For this reason, they could be used to solve Hex, or at least try. It would begin by playing out a game as both red and blue, and then work out how it could have done better for each. Then it plays out the game again, only better. It continues to refine its performance, occasionally inserting variations in its behaviour to see how it gets on. The intention would be to find those combinations of moves that could always lead to a win.

Fuzzy logic

Fuzzy logic deals with probabilities and approximations, which have not traditionally been something computers handled very well. It aims to give the computer an estimating brain. In Hex, it could be used to estimate whether the AI was building its path in the 'Right' direction, i.e building it towards the opposite edge instead of doubling back on itself like a lemon. Fuzzy logic doesn't deal too much in specific details so much as returns the probability that a move will be heading in the right direction. For a 7×7 board, fuzzy logic might seem overkill, but for larger boards it could lead to significant performance benefits.

Scripted AI

AI is commonly implemented in games using *scripting*. Instead of coding behaviour directly into the game, designers typically write script inside an external text file, telling the game how to respond and how to think at runtime. If designers want to change the behaviour after the game is compiled, they can simply re-write the script in the file and run the game again. Some of the most popular scripting languages for games are Lua and Python.

Summary

This chapter considered the AI for a simple game of Hex. In doing so it illustrated a number of AI concepts, including path finding, finite state machines, game trees and heuristic algorithms. The importance of AI in gaming cannot be understated because most games nowadays include some form of AI, whether it's the computer player in a game of Hex or an NPC in a first-person shooter. AI also looks set to become hardware accelerated, as video cards are now. This is an indication of what the future may hold for AI in gaming.

09

distribution and support

In this chapter you will learn how to:

- download and install NSIS
- use NSIS to build installation programs
- create installers for Sokoban or Hex
- provide support through forums
- create a forum and put it online

No problem can withstand the assault of sustained thinking.

Voltaire

9.1 Installers and distribution

This chapter focuses on distribution. It examines how games are installed to the user's machine, and how developers can offer support to gamers. These topics can easily be overlooked.

You've made a game. Now it's time for people to play it. There are several ways a developer can handle this situation. They can package all the game files up in a zip file and let the user download and extract them manually. The trouble is that doesn't look particularly professional. Once the game has been extracted the user needs to decide what to do. If they're experienced then it won't be a problem; just run the program. But this can be a dangerous assumption to make. Most gamers are accustomed to the luxury of an installer. This application only needs to be run once. It installs the game to the system, sets up a Start menu entry and maybe a desktop icon. That's it. And there's no reason your game can't have an installer.

NSIS – the free installer

NSIS is an acronym for *Nullsoft Scriptable Install System*. It's a free, open source program to make installation programs for your software, including games. NSIS works like a compiler. Programmers create scripts using the easy-to-learn NSIS language. These tell NSIS what files to install, what icons to make, which screens to show and so on. The NSIS compiler then generates an executable installer based on the script.

NSIS is an all-in-one package, with documentation, examples and a compiler. Download it from **http://nsis.sourceforge.net/ Main_Page,** and install.

9.2 Getting started with NSIS

Once installed, NSIS is added to the start menu and the MakeNSISW application is ready to compile some scripts. With

NSIS, each script refers to a separate installation program; one script, one installer. The script defines the behaviour of an installer – the name, what images will appear, the files to install etc. To make a NSIS script, open up a new text file in Notepad and save the file with an extension of .nsi.

Installer attributes

An NSIS script begins by defining attributes. These are properties of the installer. NSIS has a number of predefined attributes that can be specified, such as *Name*, and the default installation path. Consider the following sample lines of script.

```
; The name of the installer
Name "Sokoban Installer"
```

```
; The installation file to create
OutFile "setup.exe"
```

```
; The default installation directory
InstallDir $PROGRAMFILES\Sokoban
```

* The ; character denotes comments. These lines are ignored by the compiler.

Common attributes

The NSIS attributes take the form of <Attribute> <Value>, such as *Name "Sokoban Installer"*. Some useful attributes are listed below. All are optional, and default values are underlined.

Name (string) – the name of the installation program.

OutFile (string) – file name of the installation executable.

CRCCheck (on | off | force) – if On, a Cyclic Redundancy Check is performed at the beginning of the installation to check that it wasn't corrupted during download.

AutoCloseWindow (true | false) – specifies whether the installer closes automatically when it's completed.

XPStyle (on | off) – uses the smoother XP buttons and controls.

LicenseData (string) – if a licence page is shown (see below), this is the path to a text or RTF file where the page text is stored.

InstallDir (string) – the default directory to install to unless changed by the user. This path can include a number of predefined variables for specific system directories. Some of these include:

$PROGRAMFILES (usually C:\Program Files\).

$DESKTOP

$WINDIR

Pages

Attributes are useful for defining specific properties about the installer application itself. Pages are specific parts of the installer, the sequence of screens a user will go through as they navigate the Install wizard. Page 1 appears, they click Next and Page 2 appears, and so on. Pages come in various kinds. The directory page will prompt the user for an installation directory, and the licence page will show a EULA (end user licence agreement). Pages appear in the order they're listed in the script, e.g.

```
Page license
Page directory
Page instfiles
```

Common NSIS Pages

NSIS installers can include a range of pages, each with a different purpose. The following list summarizes some of the pages on offer – all are optional.

License – is used for showing the EULA (End User Licence Agreement). In order to install the software, users are required to click the Agree button.

Components – offers a range of installation options. The user could choose which components to install, or the options of a Minimum, Standard and Maximum installation could be offered.

Directory – lets users choose a destination directory where files are to be installed to.

Instfiles – the page where installation takes place.

Sections

A section represents a collection of files to be installed. This works hand in hand with the components page if more than one section exists. Many installations for games contain only one set of files but some have more. If more than one set exists, then it's often possible for users to choose which combination to install. For this book, only one section will be defined.

The NSIS syntax for a section is similar to a function. Each one is marked by the **Section** and **SectionEnd** keywords, and between these is a list of files to install. A section can also contain a destination path. This is relative to the selected installation directory and is essential if files are to be installed in sub-directories. Consider the following complete script to install Sokoban.

```
;----------------
; The name of the installer
Name "Sokoban"

; The file to write
OutFile "setup_sokoban.exe"

; The default installation directory
InstallDir $PROGRAMFILES\Sokoban

licensedata "lis.txt"
;----------------
; Pages
Page license
Page directory
Page instfiles
;----------------

; The stuff to install
Section "" ;No components page, name not needed

; Set output path to the installation directory.
SetOutPath $INSTDIR

; Put files there
File Complete.bmp
File Crate.bmp
```

```
File Player.bmp
File Tiles.bmp
File song.mp3
File Sokoban.exe
File bass.dll
File SDL.dll

SectionEnd ; end the section
```

9.3 Compiling NSIS scripts

The MakeNSISW application is the NSIS Compiler. It accepts scripts in .NSI format and compiles them into self-contained executable installers. Once the script is compiled, developers do not need to distribute the individual files of the game separately as they are all compressed into the installer program.

To compile a script:

1 Load **MakeNSISW**.

2 Click **Load Script**.

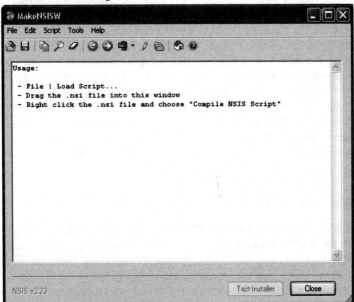

Figure 9.1 The MakeNSISW window

3 The script will be compiled automatically.

4 Any errors are reported in the text box.

5 Once compiled, click **Test Installer** to test the installer.

Enhanced installers

NSIS is a powerful tool, and sports a range of features not covered in this book. Installations can be enhanced with NSIS using skins to make them look better. Furthermore, NSIS can process and edit the registry, create and edit config files, and update and patch programs. Its scripting capabilities can control almost every aspect of an installation. Before reading on, it's worth exploring NSIS and taking a look at its more advanced features.

9.4   Setting up a game forum

A forum (or bulletin board) is something most Internet users are familiar with nowadays. It refers to online communities where Net users can read messages posted by others and can post messages themselves. Some communities are dedicated to specific topics; others are for general chit-chat. In forums, new users sign-up for an account, gain a user name and password, and can then join in. Some forums are private and can only be joined with the approval of their *moderator* or *administrator* (those who operate and maintain the forum). Most computer games have an associated forum online, which are open and public, so anybody can join. It's a place gamers can go to chat with other gamers. Sometimes it's also a place gamers go to voice their dissatisfaction and raise technical support issues, but also to get help. Some gamers even join to congratulate developers on their work, giving them warm words of encouragement.

Why use a forum?

An Internet forum is useful for gamers and developers alike. Developers who host a web forum are more likely to connect with gamers than those who do not. It can allow them to offer cost-effective support to customers, and can help to give a game maximum exposure by creating thriving communities.

An Internet forum has the following useful properties.

Technical support

Users can post their technical issues in a public place. The developer can read the forums, check out their problems and post solutions. If other users meet similar problems, they can search the forum to find previous messages with a solution. This means you get fewer duplicate mails asking the same questions.

Maximize exposure

A forum is a place where people hang out and read messages. By creating communities around your products, people can talk about your games – existing games or ones they are anticipating. In this way, forums offer a good means for making public announcements to your gamers.

Builds communities

In addition to exposure and technical support, forums can also become a place where like-minded gamers come together. It can be a place where they can make friends, meet new people, and even grow to know you as a developer.

Which forum?

Those who find the case for a forum convincing, will probably wonder how to make one. Indeed, some developers jump in and make their own home-made forum. There is a simpler way. There are a number of pre-made forum packages available for free. Developers can download the package, upload the forum files to their server and run a forum within minutes. There is a wide variety of forum packages available, including phpBB and YaBB. This book will select YaBB, and the rest of this chapter explains how to get started. YaBB is an acronym for Yet another Bulletin Board. It is easy to use, powerful, free, open source, cross-platform, secure and well documented.

Teach Yourself more

If you want to know about developing websites try HTML and PHP in the Teach Yourself series.

Downloading and preparing for YaBB

YaBB can be downloaded from **http://www.yabbforum.com/**. The download package includes the necessary files and help documentation. These should be extracted to a location on the local computer first. The package includes these directories.

♦ **cgi-bin**; this directory contains the core script files for the forum. This will eventually be uploaded to the web server.

♦ **public_html**; this directory features HTML pages. These are the default pages for the forum. They do not need to be edited, but it is possible to do so if you wish to change the look of your forum.

♦ **Quick-Guide**; the help documentation.

Customizing the scripts

Before uploading the forum files, users should check the contents of a few script files in the *cgi-bin* directory. These can be opened up in any ordinary text editor, e.g. Notepad. For YaBB to work correctly, it needs to know the Perl script path on the server. The files have been set with the default Perl script path, and most servers are likely to use this path, but some might differ. You should check with your web host to see which path their servers use. The first line in each of the script files *Adminindex.pl*, *Setup.pl*, and *YaBB.pl* features the Perl path YaBB expects. If your server is different, this line should be changed to the appropriate path. Make sure the line always starts with: #!.

Uploading YaBB

To integrate a YaBB forum with a website the forum files must first be uploaded to a web host. This is where the rest of the ordinary website files, html and images files, and so on are also hosted. The YaBB files are transferred here using an FTP application. The following steps upload a YaBB forum to a web space.

1　Using the FTP software, login to the web host using the FTP server (e.g. **ftp.mywebsite.com**). Provide a user name and password as appropriate. Please remember, YaBB can only be used on web hosts that support Perl scripts. Most commercial hosts do, but many free hosts do not.

2   On the web space, find a directory called *cgi-bin*. If it does not exist, then a directory with this name should be created. From the local computer, copy all the contents of the YaBB *cgi-bin* directory to the *cgi-bin* directory on the web host.

3   Outside of the *cgi-bin* directory on the web host, a new directory should be created; usually in *public_html*. This should be among the rest of the standard HTML pages and files for the website. Ideally, it should be called *yabbfiles*, but the name can be anything desired. From the local computer, copy the *yabbfiles* directory (inside *public_html* in the YaBB set). This should be copied to the web host inside the newly created *yabbfiles* directory.

4   Once the required files have been copied to the web host, the access privileges for these files and directories must be changed. These settings affect whether the files can be written to and read from. This process is considered next.

NOTE. More information about YaBB generally can be found in the *Quick guide* directory where YaBB was extracted.

Setting file permissions

At this point, all the forum files are uploaded to the server. Each file has a set of permissions for reading and writing, and also for whether it can be accessed at all. YaBB requires the forum files to be changed to specific settings in order to work. Each setting, read, write and execute has an integer value, and the total for any file reflects the range of settings that apply to it. In Unix/ Linux, the permissions are set with the command **chmod,** but a quicker method is to use FileZilla FTP. It's a case of selecting the file, entering a specific integer and then clicking Apply.

chmod values and file permissions

chmod values determine read and write file permissions for files on the server. For online forums like YaBB, users will write messages and have their messages recorded on the forum for others to see. Thus, some files and folders will need specific read-write permissions to allow this kind of behaviour. The chmod values determine the permissions for files. It's simple arithmetic: add together the values (4 = read, 2 = write and 1 = execute) to get a single digit to define which permissions have been granted, e.g.

6 = read and write permission. There are three digits, because there are three categories of user: the owner of the file, other members of the owner's workgroup, and everybody else. So, a chmod value of 755 means that the owner has full access, but everybody else only has read and execute permission.

Most FTP programs offer simple ways for users to specify the file permissions. The following dialog box of FileZilla (a free FTP) allows users to specify file permissions via both check boxes and chmod values.

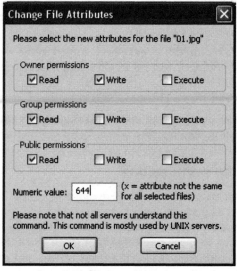

Figure 9.2 The File Attributes dialog box in FileZilla

To set file permissions:

1 Right-click one or more files and/or directories in the browser.

2 Click **File Attributes**.

3 This displays a menu where a value can be entered. This number will reflect the combination of access privileges to be applied to the file(s).

The table lists the YaBB files and directories and their corresponding permissions, given here as chmod values.

* indicates the permission applies to all the files in the directory,

cgi-bin files:

cgi-bin/yabb2	755
cgi-bin/yabb2/AdminIndex.pl	755
cgi-bin/yabb2/FixFile.pl	755
cgi-bin/yabb2/Paths.pl	666
cgi-bin/yabb2/Setup.pl	755
cgi-bin/yabb2/YaBB.pl	755
cgi-bin/yabb2/Admin	777
cgi-bin/yabb2/Admin/* (all files)	666
cgi-bin/yabb2/Boards	777
cgi-bin/yabb2/Boards/*	666
cgi-bin/yabb2/Convert	777
cgi-bin/yabb2/Convert/Boards	777
cgi-bin/yabb2/Convert/Members	777
cgi-bin/yabb2/Convert/Messages	777
cgi-bin/yabb2/Convert/Variables	777
cgi-bin/yabb2/Help/English/Admin	777
cgi-bin/yabb2/Help/English/Admin/*	777
cgi-bin/yabb2/Help/English/Gmod	777
cgi-bin/yabb2/Help/English/Gmod/*	777
cgi-bin/yabb2/Help/English/Moderator	777
cgi-bin/yabb2/Help/English/Moderator/*	777
cgi-bin/yabb2/Help/English/User	777
cgi-bin/yabb2/Help/English/User/*	777
cgi-bin/yabb2/Languages/English	777
cgi-bin/yabb2/Languages/English/*	777
cgi-bin/yabb2/Languages/English/agreement.txt	666
cgi-bin/yabb2/Languages/English/censor.txt	666
cgi-bin/yabb2/Members	777
cgi-bin/yabb2/Members/*	666
cgi-bin/yabb2/Messages	777
cgi-bin/yabb2/Messages/*	666
cgi-bin/yabb2/Modules/Digest	777
cgi-bin/yabb2/Modules/Digest/HMAC_MD5.pm	777
cgi-bin/yabb2/Modules/Digest/MD5.pm	777
cgi-bin/yabb2/Modules/Time	777
cgi-bin/yabb2/Modules/Time/HiRes.pm	777
cgi-bin/yabb2/Modules/Upload	777
cgi-bin/yabb2/Modules/Upload/CGI.pm	777
cgi-bin/yabb2/Modules/Upload/CGI	777
cgi-bin/yabb2/Modules/Upload/CGI/Util.pm	777
cgi-bin/yabb2/Sources	766

```
cgi-bin/yabb2/Sources/* (all files)              755
cgi-bin/yabb2/Templates                          766
cgi-bin/yabb2/Templates/default                  766
cgi-bin/yabb2/Templates/default/*                666
cgi-bin/yabb2/Variables                          766
cgi-bin/yabb2/Variables/*                        666
```

public_html files:

```
public_html/yabbfiles                                      777
public_html/yabbfiles/*.js                                 666
public_html/yabbfiles/Attachments                          777
public_html/yabbfiles/avatars                              777
public_html/yabbfiles/avatars/*                            666
public_html/yabbfiles/Buttons                              777
public_html/yabbfiles/Buttons/English/*                    666
public_html/yabbfiles/ModImages                            777
public_html/yabbfiles/Smilies                              777
public_html/yabbfiles/Smilies/*                            666
public_html/yabbfiles/Templates/Admin                      777
public_html/yabbfiles/Templates/Admin/default/*            666
public_html/yabbfiles/Templates/Admin/default.css          666
public_html/yabbfiles/Templates/Forum                      777
public_html/yabbfiles/Templates/Forum/default/*            666
public_html/yabbfiles/Templates/Forum/default.css          666
```

Configuring the forum

Uploading files and setting file permissions can be a long and tedious process. Once completed, however, the forum is almost ready to try. You can access the forum by navigating a web browser to *setup.pl* in the *cgi-bin*. The address will be something like: **http://www.example.com/cgi-bin/yabb2/Setup.pl**. This page provides options to configure and accept forum settings. In this section, it's important to do the following.

1 Enter a user name and password if asked. You begin as the administrator user. Your default user name will be: *admin*, and the password: *admin*. These settings should be changed as soon as possible.

2 The paths screen displays where the YaBB HTML and data files are to be located. Default settings will be entered already, and often these are correct. In specific cases, they may need to be changed.

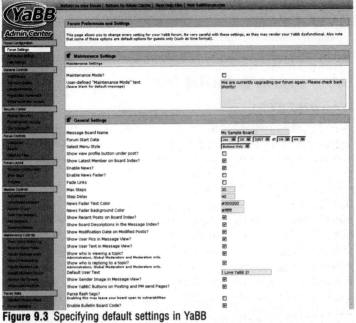

Figure 9.3 Specifying default settings in YaBB

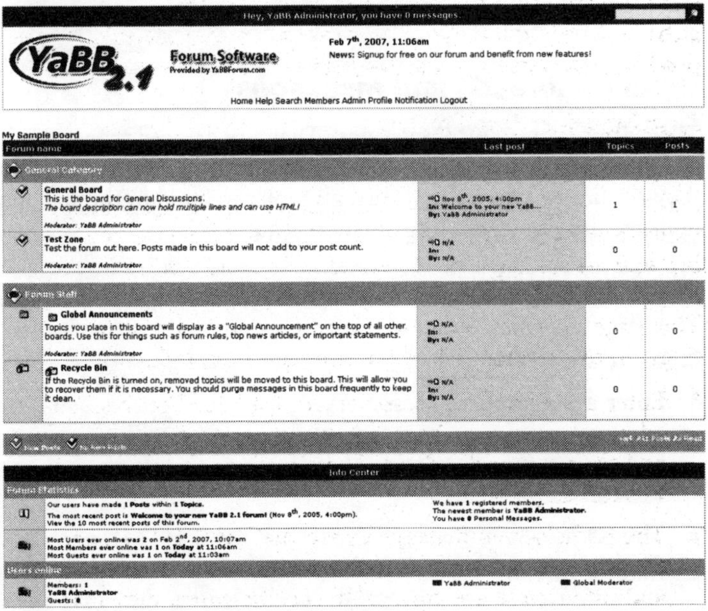

Figure 9.4 The boards on a new YaBB forum

3 Next, the localization screen allows administrators to set the time zone for the forum. After this, YaBB will perform some required checks, and then the forum is ready to use.

9.5 Using a YaBB forum

Using a YaBB forum is simple. The general forum can be logged onto via the *YaBB.pl* page, which will have an address something like: **http://www.example.com/cgi-bin/yabb2/YaBB.pl**.

Boards

A YaBB forum is made up of message boards. These allow the forum to be divided into subject areas. There might be a general space for chit-chat between users, a technical support section where people discuss technical problems with your game, and a game discussion section for people to chat about the game. A board contains threads, and threads contain messages.

A YaBB forum is created with the default boards: general, test zone, global announcements and recycle bin. These can be changed.

Creating threads and messages

Threads are topics or discussions. They are created from an initial message, a topic starter, and when other users post replies they are linked into it. This way, all replies related to the starting message are organized in a single thread.

To create a thread:

1 Enter a board.

2 Click **Start New Topic**.

3 Enter a **Subject** and **Message**.

4 Click **Post**.

To reply in a thread:

1 Enter a board.

2 Enter a thread.

3 Click **Reply**.

4 Enter a **Message**.

5 Click **Post**.

Admin control

The forum administrators can do more than the average user and are responsible for forum maintenance. They can create new boards, revoke a user's membership, make boards private, and so on. To access the admin settings, log in as the administrator and click the **Admin** button in the top row of options. Here are some of the things an administrator do.

Add and remove boards

The admin user can add and remove boards from the forum. This is useful if you want to change the default settings and add some new boards related specifically to your software.

To add a board:

1 Click **Admin** to enter the Admin Center.

2 Click **Forum Controls > Boards**.

3 To add one board enter 1 in the **Add or Edit Boards** text box.

4 Click **Add**.

5 Fill in the form. Give the board a name, and a unique ID.

6 Click **Save**. The new board is now created.

To remove a board:

1 Click **Admin** to enter the Admin Center.

2 Click **Forum Controls > Boards**.

3 This screen shows a list of boards. Tick the ones to be deleted.

4 Tick **Remove** in the **With Selected** check box.

5 Click **Go**.

Word censorship

YaBB offers the ability to censor specific words, which it does by substitution. If a user uses a censored word in a message, the forum will substitute it for whatever you have specified. YaBB comes with a default censorship scheme, and this can be changed.

To view and edit censorship settings:

1 Click **Admin** to enter the Admin Center.

2 Click **General Controls > Censored Words**.

3 Edit the list using the form: censored_word=substitute_word.

Edit members

Members are the people who join your forum. They will typically be gamers. They will be able to post and read messages, but they do not have administrator access.

To view or delete members:

1 Click **Admin** to enter the Admin Center.

2 Click **Member Controls > View/Delete Members**.

3 This displays a list of all members registered with the forum. You can click a member's name to view their details.

4 To delete a member, enter a tick on the **Delete** check box for all members to be removed, and click **Delete Members**.

Summary

This chapter showed how to create an installation package for games and set up a forum for gamers. The installation package is important because it makes the distribution of games simpler, both for developers and gamers. Installation programs are one of the first impressions gamers have of a game. Thus, it's important to make a good first impression. A forum offers all kinds of other benefits to developers and gamers, including technical support, social tools and a place to discuss your games.

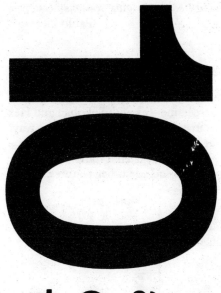

10

action effects and techniques

Computers are useless. They can only give you answers.
Pablo Picasso

10.1 Game characters

This chapter takes a look at games programming generally.
Rather than create a complete game – as with Sokoban and Hex
– it looks at specific features in existing games and explores ways
to implement them in your own games. It begins by taking a
look at game characters – the player, enemies and other game
objects. From there it expands to include other features.

Figure 10.1 A game character and its attributes

Game characters refer to all the creatures and units that may
feature in a game. Sokoban only had one character, but most
games have many more. An RTS (Real Time Strategy) game,
like *Command & Conquer 3*, typically allows you to recruit
hundreds of units from different dwellings. A platform game
also has many characters – the player themselves, and all the
enemies featured throughout a level. The different characters
usually belong in various categories – like 'Evil Wizard', and
'Barbarian', and a level may contain many enemies from each
category. Thus, each category is a character class, and each appearance of a character in a level is an instance of a specific
class, e.g. Wizard 1 and Wizard 2 are instances of the Wizard
class. This might initially seem to go without saying, but encap-
sulating characters as classes is important for game design. This
is because: it simplifies the design and makes editing code easier;

its modularity makes it easy to add or remove characters; and new characters can be derived from old ones, inheriting their behaviour. Class design is also important for establishing relationships between characters, as shown later. In general, all the characters featured in a game will be derived from a common ancestor class. This abstract class represents the minimum set of properties and methods a character *must* have. The following C++ code features a sample base class for characters in a side-scrolling action platform game.

Sample code

```cpp
class cCharacter
{
  private:
  protected:
    int m_XPos;
    int m_YPos;
    int m_Width;
    int m_Height;
    std::string m_ClassType;
    DWORD m_Color;
    bool m_Visible;
    CResource *m_Surface;
  public:
    int m_Health;
    int m_Damage;
};
```

Code discussion

The above base class for characters will be the starting point for many games. From this class, many other kinds of characters can be derived. This base class contains a number of crucial properties, some of which are discussed below.

m_XPos, m_YPos, m_Width, m_Height

These are dimensions of the character. The X and Y pos refer to the pixel position of the character, usually measured from the top left corner *of the level* – not of the screen. Many levels are too large to fit on screen, meaning the 'camera' scrolls as the player moves through a level. The camera is a window looking onto only a portion of the level. So in most games, character positions are specified relative to the level origin, and not the screen origin. The coordinate space of a level is called *World Space*, or *Global Space*. Programming scrollable levels themselves is considered on page 160.

CResource *m_Surface

This is a pointer to the graphic resource for the character, such as an SDL_Surface pointer. This is the actual character graphic. In Chapter 6, a resource manager was created for Sokoban to ensure no duplicate resources were loaded into memory. For this reason, resources are loaded independently of the game characters, which only deal with pointers from the resource manager for their graphics.

m_Health, m_Damage

Health represents the HP (Hit Points) of a character instance, often 100 is the maximum. At 100, the character is in good health, and at 0 it is eliminated. *Damage* represents the damage this character inflicts upon another's health in a single attack. This value might be somewhere between 5 and 10.

• All of these character properties will change and update during the game loop, as the action unfolds.

10.2   Motion and transformation

The previous section demonstrated how game characters can be encapsulated into classes that encode position, size, colour and other properties. However, this strategy need not only apply to characters. Other objects like tables, chairs, and projectiles also have appearance, position and size in a level. From this it follows that any movable object in a level can be derived from the character base class. For inanimate objects, the health property represents the durability of an object, and damage represents the injury it causes when it strikes another object or character. From here onwards, then, game characters and other objects will collectively be termed a *game object*. This section examines the motion of game objects in a level.

Vectors

Imagine a spaceship shooter game, viewed from a top-down view, i.e. one looking straight down at the space ship, and at other enemies and asteroids, etc. The left and right keys rotate the player's spaceship around its centre of gravity to face different directions. The forward key moves the spaceship forwards along the direction it is facing. Initially, this spaceship movement might appear as though it can be handled just through adding and subtracting its X or Y position. This is because adding or subtracting on the Y axis moves the spaceship up and down, and adding or subtracting on the X axis moves the spaceship left and right. But what happens if the spaceship is facing a 33° angle, and then the player presses forwards? Here, movement occurs on both axes disproportionately. To solve this, developers use *vectors* to encode direction.

Like standard coordinates, vectors have an X and Y component, but rather than represent an absolute position from the origin, vectors define displacement from any arbitrary location. Consider Figure 10.2.

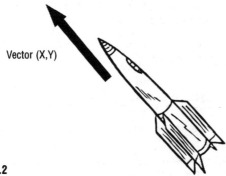

Vector (X,Y)

Figure 10.2

The vector (3,3) doesn't *necessarily* mean move *from the origin* by 3 on the X axis and by 3 on the Y axis. This displacement could be measured from any coordinate on the grid. Vectors have two important properties:

- **Direction** – e.g. (3,3) represents a 45° displacement by 3 units on each axis. The reverse direction to this would be (-3,-3).

- **Magnitude** – the length of the vector, which corresponds to the hypotenuse of a right-angled triangle. The length can be calculated using Pythagoras Theorem, as follows:

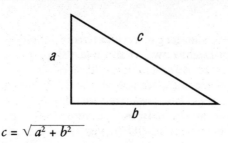

$$c = \sqrt{a^2 + b^2}$$

Where a and b are the opposite and adjacent sides of the right-angled triangle, and c is the hypotenuse. For the purposes of this book it is enough to know that magnitude represents the length of the diagonal.

Unit vectors and scaling

Before vectors can be applied to moving a spaceship or other game object, it's necessary to consider scaling and unit vectors.

Scaling

When a vector is scaled, it is multiplied. That is, each of its X and Y components are multiplied by the same number. To make a vector twice as large, it is multiplied by 2. So (3,3) becomes (6,6). And to scale a vector by half, it is multiplied by 0.5. So (3,3) becomes (1.5,1.5). The multiplier is called the *scaling factor*. Scaling is useful for increasing or decreasing the magnitude of a vector, and therefore changing the displacement in any particular direction. Notice, that scaling a vector does not change vector direction – unless it is multiplied by a negative scaling factor (opposite direction). So scaling changes magnitude, and this affects how much displacement there is in any direction.

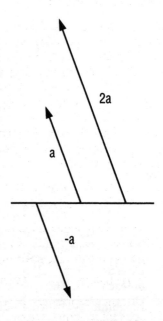

Figure 10.3 Scaling vectors

Unit vector

Vectors such as (3,3) and (6,6) or (7,2) all
represent a direction and have magnitude.
However, a vector whose magnitude is 1 is
a special kind of vector, called a unit vector
(see Figure 10.4). This has no magnitude,
only direction. It's the equivalent of pointing in a direction and saying 'That way',
without specifying how far someone needs
to travel. The beauty of this is, by knowing
only direction, you can scale the unit vector
by any distance to travel in that direction.
The result of scaling will be a vector with a
specified displacement in that direction. For
this reason, a unit vector is also called a *direction vector*. To calculate a unit vector (to
normalize), it should be divided by its magnitude.

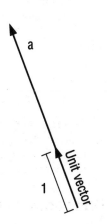

Figure 10.4

Moving with vectors

So how does a spaceship get to move with vectors? In a space
shooter game, the spaceship is derived from a game object, which
has a position (X, Y) in the game world. The spaceship also has
direction, encoded in a unit vector. As it is rotated by pressing
left or right, it turns to face new directions. Then, when the
forward key is pressed, it begins to travel (at a constant speed)
from its current location towards a direction (vector direction),
across a specific distance (vector magnitude) within a period of
time (in milliseconds). To move the spaceship, then, the following key events occur.

1 The distance/speed/time formula states that:

   ```
   Distance = Speed x Time
   ```

   Time is often measured in milliseconds during the game loop
   between each frame. So, given a speed of, say 5 units per
   frame, the distance to travel in any given frame might be:

   ```
   Distance = 5 * (time in milliseconds)
   ```

2 Distance represents how far in the current direction the
   spaceship must travel for this frame. To generate an
   appropriate vector displacement, the direction vector of the

spaceship should be scaled by the distance to travel. The resulting vector should then be added to the current position of the spaceship. Consider this, called once on each frame.

```
void update()
{
  if(forward_key_pressed==TRUE)
  {
    DWORD time = GetTimeSinceLastFrame();
    float Speed = 5.0f;
    float Distance = Speed * time;

    point Result = DirVector * Distance;

    spaceship.pos += Result;
  }
}
```

> For a more complete description of vectors please see *Teach Yourself Mathematics*.

10.3 Collision detection

When two objects intersect, they are said to collide. A bullet fired from a gun may collide with an enemy character on its trajectory, meaning the character got hit. Similarly, as the player moves around a level they may collide with walls and other solid objects. Upon colliding, the player should be prevented from moving any further in that direction – they shouldn't be able to pass through walls. Collision detection, the process of determining when collisions happen, is particularly important for games.

Bounding areas

A level may contain many moving objects. This means there's the potential for many collisions to occur simultaneously. The game loop must therefore check each object in turn and test whether it collides with another.

Consider the two objects in Figure 10.5. The most accurate way to test for a collision between them would be to scan through all the pixels in the first image and compare them to the pixels in

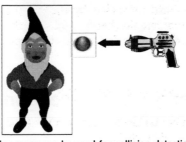

Figure 10.5 Bounding areas can be used for collision detection

the second. If any pixels overlap, then there is a collision. But, there's a problem with this method. Given that a level may contain hundreds of game objects with hundreds of pixels each, and given that collision detection occurs on every frame, pixel by pixel comparisons would bring the game to a standstill on most home computers. In short, it'd be too much processing. To solve this, game developers start by approximating the size of a game object using a *bounding rectangle* which encloses it completely. (For 3D, it's a *bounding box*.) A bounding rectangle is assigned to every game object, and collisions are tested by comparing them, and not pixels. This method is only an approximation of collision, but it proves an effective enough strategy for games.

Sometimes developers will use other shapes, such as circles and spheres, as well as rectangles and boxes for collision detection.

Comparing bounding rectangles

Testing for a collision involves comparing two bounding rectangles. If they intersect, there is a collision. The following C++ function accepts two rectangles as an argument, compares them and returns true or false reflecting whether they intersect.

```
bool areIntersecting(RECT a, RECT b)
{
  RECT intersect;
  intersect.left = max(a.left, b.left);
  intersect.top = max(a.top, b.top);
  intersect.right = min(a.right, b.right );
  intersect.bottom = min(a.bottom, b.bottom);

  if(intersect.right > intersect.left &&
    intersect.bottom > intersect.top)
```

```
      return true;
  else
      return false;
}
```

10.4 Scene management and hierarchies

Often objects have a relationship with each other and are not independent in terms of their position and size. Imagine a level that contains a giant conveyor belt. On the belt is a car, and inside the car is a passenger. The belt has its own position within the level, and so does the car and so does the passenger. But if the belt moves, both the car and the passenger inside will move accordingly because their position is dependent on the belt. Similarly, if the belt was to remain motionless and only the car moved, then the passenger would move with the car, but the belt would be unaffected. This kind of dependency, between the belt, the car and the passenger, is called a *hierarchical relationship*.

Scene nodes and hierarchies

A hierarchy can be visualized as a tree, as shown in Figure 10.6. The topmost node is called the *root node* (or *ultimate parent*) and those beneath are called *child* nodes. Any nodes above a

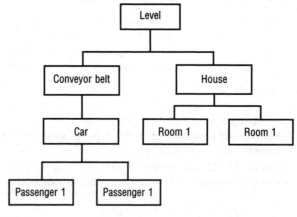

Figure 10.6

child are *parent* nodes because child nodes belong to a parent. Any nodes belonging to the same parent are called *sibling* nodes. Using a hierarchical structure, the relationship between objects throughout the level can be described. In the case of positioning objects – say the belt, car and passenger – the following applies: Every node's position is relative to its parent. For example, the belt might be situated at the origin of the level (0,0). The car's position is at (5,5) – the car is a child of the belt. Likewise, the passenger may have a position of (1,1), but that is relative from the car, and not the origin. In effect, the passenger is (1,1) away from the car origin; meaning it is at (6,6) in the level. So each node has two positions; a *relative* and an *absolute* position. The relative position describes its offset from the parent node, and the absolute position is its acumulative position in the level.

Implementing hierarchies

Encoding hierarchical relationships between game objects involves creating a SceneNode class. This class maintains two std::vector arrays.

* A list of pointers to all the game objects belonging to this node. In other words, if the node is transformed, all attached scene objects will be affected.

* A list of SceneNode pointers that are children of this node. This way, every node keeps track of its children, and its children's children, recursively through the hierarchy. Consider the following C++ code.

```
class cSceneNode
{
  private:
  protected:
  public:

    //characters attached to node
    std::vector<cCharacter*> m_SceneObjects;

    //List of child nodes
    std::vector<cSceneNode*> m_ChildNodes;
};
```

10.5   Layers and Z ordering

In a side-scrolling platform game, the world will usually adhere
to the 'rules of perception'. That is, objects nearer the front –
closer to the camera – will appear in front of those in the background. Objects at the front obscure those behind them, unless
the foreground object is made from glass or mist, etc. (see Figure 10.7). The process of drawing objects in order of distance,
or Z order, is known as the painter's algorithm, which we first
met in Chapter 6.

Figure 10.7

Ordering layers

Layers are like the clear acetate sheets used in drawn cartoons,
and they are stacked on top of one another. The layer will have
a position, and width and height, but it's completely transparent. Its purpose is to organize a set of game objects together on
a single layer for drawing. In this way, layers can be stacked on
top of each other to form a scene with depth. All foreground
objects will be on the top layer, and all background objects are
on the bottom layer, and there will be a variety of depths in-
between. The job of a render manager is to draw the level to the
display on each frame, cycling through the layers and drawing
each one. Starting at the back and moving forwards layer by
layer to ensure background objects are drawn first, and foreground objects are drawn over them. The foreground layer will

have a Z order of 0, and each layer behind will have an incrementally higher Z order.

Implementing layers

Creating layers in a game is similar to creating hierarchies of objects. A layer object needs to be created. A render manager will maintain a std::vector list of layers, in their Z order. Each layer object will maintain a list of pointers to the objects belonging to the layer.

Consider the following C++ code.

```cpp
class cLayer
{
  private:
  protected:
  public:

  //Layer Current Z-Order
  int m_ZOrder;
  RECT m_LayerDimensions;

  //Scene Objects attached to this layer
  std::vector<cCharacter*> m_SceneObjects;

  void draw()
  {
    //draws all objects on this layer

    for(unsigned int i=0; i<m_SceneObjects.size();
      i++)
    {
      m_SceneObjects[i]->draw();
    }
  }
};

//Other code here...
[...]

//Function to draw layers in Z-Order
//Called during game loop
```

```
void draw(std::vector<cLayer*> Layers)
{
  //List arranged in z-order

  for(unsigned int i=0; i<Layers.size(); i++)
  {
    //draws the layer

    Layers[i]->draw();
  }
}
```

10.6   Frustum and culling

There's a lot going on in a game. During one cycle of the game loop, a game must process all the objects in a level, the object relationships, collision detection mechanisms, layers, and more, so optimization techniques are important for game performance. It's about finding ways of reducing overheads to speed up processing time.

One of most important and successful optimizations a game can perform is *culling*. In any game level there will be many objects drawn to the display. For a platformer, this will include platforms, enemies, guns, power-ups, buildings and more. Much of the level – in fact, most – will not be visible to the player in any given frame, but will be 'off-stage'. What the player sees is 'on-stage', a subset of the level. As the screen scrolls, new off-stage areas are brought into view while once on-stage areas disappear. However, even though most of the level is off-stage, graphics libraries like SDL, DirectX or OpenGL will still attempt to draw all that off-stage data. They will not make checks to determine whether their graphics are actually viewable on screen or not. That's the responsibility of the developer.

Drawing frustum graphics

Graphics that are on-stage are said to be in the *frustum* (see Figure 10.8). This represents what the camera sees, so off-stage data is outside its scope. The process of culling involves drawing only data that is in the frustum. In doing this, a game can reduce its processing by not drawing what can't be seen. That doesn't

CULLED

(0,0)

FRUSTUM

Figure 10.8 The frustrum

mean ignoring off-screen data completely. Games still process
all the events and transformations that occur, but culling means
ignoring off-screen data in the context of drawing.

The process is similar to collision detection. Rather than testing
collisions between bounding rectangles of objects in a level, culling is tested between the frustum rectangle and layer rectangles.
The frustum rectangle corresponds to the width and height of
the game window, and the X and Y pos will vary depending on
where in the level the frustum has scrolled to. Layers also have a
(X,Y) position, and width and height. If the frustum rectangle
intersects a layer rectangle, then that layer and its contents are
drawn.

Implementing culling

After encountering collision detection and layers, culling can be
implemented almost effortlessly.

Consider the following C++ code sample, taken from the render
function of the game loop.

```cpp
void update()
{
  //Rectangle for viewing Frustum
  RECT Frustum;

  //Test against frustum
  for(unsigned int i=0; i<Layers.size(); i++)
```

```
    {
        Layers->m_Visible=false;

        //If intersects frustum
        if(areIntersecting(Frustum, Layers[i]->
          m_LayerDimensions))
        Layers->m_Visible=true;
    }
}
```

10.7 Parallax scrolling

The frustum represents the region of a level that is visible on screen. To bring new regions into view, the level must scroll. The speed at which layers move is known as the scroll rate (or speed). The issue of scrolling introduces a useful technique adopted by many side-scrolling games. It's known as *parallax scrolling* and it's designed to enhance the depth of 2D environments.

Parallax scrolling ensures that different layers scroll at different speeds, proportionally to their distance from the camera. Layers with lower Z orders (those closer to the front) scroll past the frustum faster than layers behind them. The background layer, therefore, is the slowest layer to scroll and the foreground layer is the fastest. The purpose behind this optical illusion is to create a sense of depth to a scene; to enhance the realism of 2D games. It reinforces the idea that foreground objects are closer and background ones are further away.

NOTE. Scrolling layers is achieved using the same principles as moving a spaceship or some other game object. Each layer has a different speed, and a direction vector specifies in which direction a layer ought to scroll.

10.8 Particle systems

Games boast a fancy range of special effects too. Some of them include: fire, explosions, fog, rain, snow and dust. First, let's consider rain, snow and other effects dealing with small particles. Rain in computer games can greatly enhance the realism of a world, even though it tends to be crudely implemented (for example, some games let you stand under shelter but it will still be raining on you!). These kinds of effects – whether done properly or not – are created by particle systems. They work on a loop by continually emitting lots of tiny textures (of a raindrop or snowflake) from the air, pulling them to the ground under the effects of gravity. Each raindrop or snowflake that hits the ground is dispersed and regenerated in the air again.

Particle systems have the following core components.

◆ **Emitter** – this is invisible, but represents a range of space, a rectangle, or circle, etc. where new particles are generated.

◆ **Particle** – a single snowflake, or a raindrop, or whatever. It's a texture, and a particle system will emit lots of them from the emitter. Once emitted, it comes under the influence of an *Affector*. A particle also has a lifetime, i.e. how long it survives before being deleted.

◆ **Affector** – the physics behind the particle system. Once particles are emitted, this controls their behaviour. It tells the particle how to behave, how to move, where to go and what happens to it. A rain or snow affector will pull the particles to the ground, but a fairy dust affector will make them dance around in the air, for example.

Figure 10.9 Fairy dust

Implementing particle systems

Particle systems typically involve two classes; a particle class, and the particle system class. The former is a 2D texture – a sprite, or a surface that represents the particles to be emitted. The latter is often created as a base class so differing kinds of particle systems, with different affectors and emitters, can be created. Particle systems are applied in the next chapter.

10.9 Explosions and atmosphere

The next special effects to consider are explosions, something lots of games feature. If a spaceship gets shot down, or an oil tanker goes up in flames, suddenly the game object becomes submerged in an explosion. In most 2D games, explosions are a partially transparent sprite. They are an animated 2D surface (*billboard*). In addition to being an animated surface, a sprite is attached to a layer in the scene and expanded and shrunk dynamically, to emphasize the effect (see Figure 10.10). At the apex of the explosion, the sprite is scaled to perhaps twice its size, and then it peters out, gradually shrinking into oblivion. This cunning strategy need not apply merely to explosions, of course. It can be applied to fog, haze and other kinds of similar effects. The next chapter will explain further how this technique can be applied.

Scaled billboard

Figure 10.10

Summary

This chapter has considered a number of important techniques that apply to games more generally. We have looked at game characters, movement, collision detection, scene hierarchies, layers, culling and particle systems.

11

designing
Action-Bot

In this chapter you will learn:

- how to design an end-of-level boss
- how to apply billboards and particle systems
- about skeletal animation

Game characters don't have to really be intelligent. They just need to avoid doing stupid things in front of the player.

John Carmack

11.1 Introducing Action-Bot

This chapter builds on the previous ones, and uses hierarchies, bounding rectangles, particle systems, layers and billboards to design an end-of-level (or end-of-book) boss. This hypothetical boss will be called 'Action-Bot', and it will feature in an equally hypothetical action game, called *Ludicrous Gibs*. (Gibs is an abbreviation for giblets, which describes the flesh, bones, and bloodied bits of gore that often fly around levels of a computer game.) This book does not include working code for the Boss — that is an exercise for the reader. But it will examine how many of the previously explained techniques come together into a working whole.

Figure 11.1

This end-of-level boss is a large, tough and well-armed enemy. It's the kind of creature the player encounters at the end of a level, or at a critical stage in the game. The boss, Action-Bot, is featured in Figure 11.1. Please excuse my cliché drawing, but there are two properties about Action-Bot worth noting.

- **Action-Bot has two weapons** – one on each arm; a plasma cannon that fires a continuous bolt of energy, and a stun weapon. This fires small particles that temporarily render the player motionless and vulnerable to attack.

- **Modular anatomy** – during combat with Action-Bot, each limb sustains damage separately. For example, if the plasma cannon arm is destroyed, it falls off, but Action-Bot may continue fighting with only one arm. The entire Action-Bot is destroyed only when all limbs have been destroyed.

11.2 Designing the limbs

The anatomy of Action-Bot is a hierarchy of limbs. Each limb – arm, leg, head, etc. – is a separate game object, derived from a character base class (as discussed in the previous chapter). Each limb has a (X,Y) position, and width and height. Furthermore, each limb is part of a hierarchy, meaning some limb nodes will have child limbs whose position and orientation are relative to their parent. In effect, this represents the skeletal structure of the character. For example, if the upper arm moves, so will the lower arm, and in turn, so will the hand. This is because the upper arm is the parent of the lower, and the lower arm is the parent of the hand. Consider Figure 11.2.

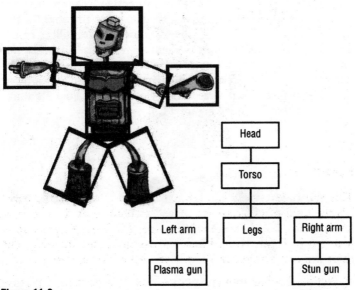

Figure 11.2

The hierarchy therefore has important implications for Action-Bot. These are listed as follows.

- **Anatomical structure** – the hierarchy keeps Action-Bot held together. Without it, its limbs would be a jumbled mess.

- **Relational motion** – the hierarchy sets strict rules about how the limbs work together, how they can move and their relationship to one another. All positions and orientations are relative to parent nodes.

- **Sustaining damage** – the hierarchy is the key to how Action-Bot sustains damage inflicted by the player. Each game object – each limb – has a health property inherited from the base class. So, if the player inflicts enough damage on the upper arm, it becomes broken and disconnected from the main torso and falls to the ground. The skeletal structure is broken. In turn, the upper arm's dependent nodes will follow – the lower arm and hand. This kind of bodily relationship is known as *skeletal animation*.

11.3 The plasma cannon

The plasma cannon is Action-Bot's offensive weapon. It fires a continuous bolt of energy and causes damage to any object within range. Implementing the plasma cannon involves billboard layers. The energy bolt graphic is a texture resource. As the cannon is fired, the energy bolt appears in front of the barrel and remains as long as the trigger is being pulled, or until the cannon's energy is depleted. But since Action-Bot is a mean boss, its ammo never expires. Consider Figure 11.3.

Figure 11.3

The energy bolt is a textured surface, and it's also a child node of the cannon. This is so that, if the arm moves or rotates at the joint, the energy bolt will always remain relative to the barrel of the cannon. There are some important properties to consider regarding the cannon.

- **Pulsating transformation** – to make the energy beam more realistic, it slowly pulsates. It throbs; growing slightly larger, then slightly smaller. This effect is achieved through a scaling transformation, interpolating between a factor of 1.5 and 1.

- **Range** – the range determines which objects are damaged when the cannon is fired. In the case of the cannon, the range can be represented by the bounding rectangle of the energy bolt object. Any objects intersecting the bolt are damaged.

11.4   The stun gun

Consider Figure 11.4. The stun gun is an immobilizer. It causes no damage, but it renders the player motionless for a limited period of time. This is useful in combination with the plasma cannon because it means Action-Bot can sustain an attack while the player is immobilized. The stun gun fires a rectangular region of fairy dust. It drifts about in the air, and then disperses.

Figure 11.4

One of the best ways to implement the stun gun, therefore, is by a particle system. Each particle of dust is a graphic specifically designed, and is an example of a *point sprite*. The gun fires an array of point sprites from an emitter, into a region controlled by an affector, where they float about. This region is represented by a bounding rectangle, and this can be tested against the player for a collision. If a collision occurred, then the player is immobilized, otherwise nothing occurs. Note, the particle system is a child node of the gun, to ensure it remains relatively positioned.

Summary

The foundation for an end-of-level boss has been illustrated but it needs a lot more work. For example, it needs Artificial Intelligence to determine how it behaves when in combat with the player. It needs to work out when to attack, when to defend and when to search for power-ups and health restores. Further to this, a number of features like rocket boots could be added – boots that allow Action-Bot to hover. To achieve this, flame billboards would be added to the bottom of its feet when it took off, and so on.

12 the games industry

In this chapter you will learn about:

- the games industry
- jobs and business
- accessibility in games
- the psychology of games

*Let your sympathies and your compassion be always with
the under dog in the fight – this is magnanimity; but bet
on the other one – this is business.*

Mark Twain

12.1 Working in the industry

This chapter rounds up the world of games programming by
exploring the games industry, looking at how to get started. For
example, how to get a job making games and how to run your
own game development company. Also, it looks at some of the
challenges which face computer games nowadays.

People looking to join the games industry usually have one of
two aims: either to get a job as a programmer in an established
development team, or to run their own business making games.
Sometimes there is a fine distinction between the two. People
who've worked in the industry for years often leave their jobs to
go it alone. This chapter looks at both approaches, but it isn't
intended to be a definitive guide or a 'guarantee of success'. There
is no such thing. The advice is just intended to be helpful for
those unsure about how to get started.

The profile of a games programmer

Games development companies find their programmers through
a variety of means. The most obvious is through job listings; or
through agencies, but this is not the only route. Some programmers have been appointed internally from other positions, perhaps as game testers, or level designers. Typically, a company
will look for a number of qualities and skills in a candidate.
They almost always make requirements about education, and
often about experience too. The important thing for a candidate
is not only to have these qualities, but to openly demonstrate
them to an employer on a CV and at interview. So what kinds of
attributes should a games programmer have?

Education

There are few companies which don't have some educational
requirements. Most require a degree in a computer-related subject, typically computer science, information systems, maths and

computing, software engineering or even business studies. Companies sometimes make exceptions to candidates without a degree, provided their experience proves equivalent knowledge. Choosing an appropriate degree should be considered carefully. I would recommend maths and computing, since both subjects feature strongly in games programming. There are also a number of universities which offer games programming degrees too.

Experience

Experience matters in the games industry. Some of the largest games companies will require significant previous experience. This means you will have worked on previous games, either with other companies or independently. For a games developer, knowledge of DirectX and OpenGL is valuable experience especially for PC games. A good course of action is to make games during your degree, if you're able. This means you'll leave university with a degree and experience combined.

Personal qualities

A potential employer will always be interested in a number of personal qualities, particularly, the ability to work well in teams, and good communication skills – your grasp of English, oral and written. Though games programming doesn't involve essay writing, you will often be required to write comments for code and to document your work clearly. And last but certainly not least, it's good if you have an interest in computer games. That doesn't mean you have to play all the latest games or develop an unhealthy game addiction, but it does mean that you aren't likely to find games programming boring. Some people enter the industry simply because they believe it'll make them lots of money. Often, these people underestimate the work involved.

12.2 Games as a business

As well as those seeking jobs in the industry, there will be others going it alone as a business. It might not strictly be alone in the sense of one person, and may involve a small team of people in business, but regardless of numbers, a different set of challenges face a business compared to working as an employee. In the games industry there are many opportunities, but also many risks.

Time and investment

Time is a commodity when making games for money. Several years ago, making games was an expensive pursuit in terms of both time and money. Now this need not be the case. Computers are more affordable and many game-creating technologies are too. Products like Flash and Director aren't cheap, but they frequently prove themselves to be good investments. Libraries like SDL, DirectX, OpenGL are all free, for both commercial and non-commercial use. For the fledging game developer, cost will be important, but with the right attitude and technologies it's possible to make good games cheaply.

Skill up

Working for yourself doesn't require specific educational background and experience, but this doesn't mean those factors aren't important. On the contrary, game development requires that you know about computers, business, the industry and everything else games entail. It's important, then, to learn about game making. Books like these can really help developers get started on the right track. In addition to books, however, motivation, enthusiasm and creativity are important.

Publishers

Nowadays, publishers aren't the only route to selling games. Publishers will box, advertise and distribute games, but they will only accept certain products and usually want a hefty return for their investments. You might consider the prospect of selling games online via a website or through gaming portals. Many independent developers adopt this method with some success. Users log on, pay for the games via credit card, and then download and play.

12.3   Psychology and games

Games are said to be addictive. Indeed, those who play them often agree they are, especially when playing with friends. In recent times, computer games have been studied in scientific ways by sociologists and psychologists. The aim of many studies was to determine whether computer games had dangerous social influences, particularly on children. This question is now considered more closely.

Aggression and games

Statistically, violent crimes have increased in the UK, and many of those convicted are young people. Since most computer games are played by youth, some have tried to link the increase in crime with computer games generally. Games like *Mortal Kombat*, *Night Trap* and *Grand Theft Auto* have been among those which activists have campaigned to censor. But can games featuring violence and blood really cause people to be violent themselves? The answer is much debated. In 2002, a study called 'Aggression and psychopathology in adolescents with a preference for violent electronic games' was carried out to answer the question (published in *Aggressive Behavior*, Vol. 28, Wiley-Liss). The results were interesting. The study found a link between video games and depression, and a link with emotional difficulties, but no correspondence between computers and violence could be established. The interpretation of these results are hotly debated, and the controversy surrounding games continues.

Dangerous games!

In 2005, there were at least two recorded deaths related to games. The gamers were alleged to have played consecutively for several days without breaks.

Social development and children

Psychologists have also researched the effects games have on children's social behaviour. Critics argue that games encourage antisocial attitudes, mainly because fewer children play outside with others, and instead remain indoors at the computer. From this, there are concerns about their level of social activity. There is evidence it may have an effect later in life on how they relate to other people. In reply, some pro-gamers say it's the parents' responsibility to monitor the time children spend on games. They also debate the level of influence violent games have, and suggest violence is due to a biological predisposition. Other pro-gamers suggest that games *can* encourage social interaction. To corroborate this, they refer to multiplayer games where players across the globe, from different cultures, play together. Inevitably, anti-game activists question the validity of this argument when so many games encourage violence and competition towards other players. Some pro-gamers have even gone so far as to advocate that aggression, competition and individualism in games are necessary qualities to encourage in a competitive world!

Legalities and censorship

Games have also caused legal disputes. *Grand Theft Auto: San Andreas*, for example, was banned in Australia due to sexual content. Sometimes names needed to changed. And sometimes gruesome games like *Mortal Kombat*, *Carmageddon* and others have needed to censor blood when released in specific territories. Sometimes they removed blood completely, and other times they coloured blood green to pretend it was slime, or whatever. Much of the pressure to censor games has come from anti-game activists and religious groups who believe games to be morally dangerous. More recently in China, inventive new measures have been proposed to cap the time children can spend playing games. They do this by programming a 'fatigue technique' into games. This works by allowing normal play during the first three consecutive hours, after which the player's abilities are reduced, making them weaker than before. The longer a person plays, the weaker they become. To restore their character back to full power, featuring all the usual abilities as before, they must leave a period of no less than five hours before returning to the game.

12.4 Accessibility and games

In the world of games, developers should understand the needs of gamers. This is especially true for gamers with specialized needs, such as people with disabilities. Features that target users with disabilities are called *accessibility features*. However, it's an unfortunate fact that accessibility in games is usually neglected and inadequate. More often than not, this is because developers fail to realize its importance and how to go about achieving it in games. Both the Game Accessibility Group, and the Game Accessibility Project have a keen interest in making developers more aware about the needs of people with disabilities. Indeed, often disabilities are created by games – that is, where they could offer accessibility features, but do not. These games could have *enabled* some users, but instead they *disabled* them.

Subtitles

In every scene where there is sound there should be the option for subtitles. Not just for speaking, though. Sometimes it's important to hear other sounds in games too. The sound of a door unlocking or the sound of an enemy moving nearby.

Auditory feedback

There are estimated to be over 50 kinds of visual impairment ranging from total blindness to colour blindness. Even colour blindness comes in various forms. Some people see only in shades of grey, while others cannot distinguish between specific colours. For this reason, audio feedback from games is important. This doesn't mean that everything makes a sound in the game, which could be quite confusing. But it does mean sound is played at key times, and in response to meaningful actions, e.g. when the player jumps, or shoots a weapon, or takes damage. More subtly, sounds could be made when menu options are highlighted and clicked, and so on.

Input devices for physical disabilities

On the PC, there are many kinds of input devices for users with disabilities. Thankfully, many of these devices simulate mouse movements and key presses. This means as long as your game supports mouse and keyboard, it will also transparently support other devices too. Accessibility hardware includes the mouth controller and the head tracker.

12.5   The future of games

In terms of a big business economy, the future of games looks promising. Recent times have seen the growth of multinational publishers and also the decline of smaller developers in high street stores, but the marketplace for games is slowly moving online.

This trend explains the recent burst of new development teams selling their games online. Nowadays, games are not just the products of big business, but also the creations of individuals and small teams working from home. The most recent consoles also support online play, and look set to support online selling.

Buy-now games

The current standard way of purchasing games is a *buy-now* system. The customer pays once and receives the game – either in the shops, through mail-order or download – and no further payment is required, that is the gamer purchases ownership of the game by a DVD or CD-ROM. If a game is cheaper than the competition, then people might consider it a bargain. But if it is too cheap, this might lead customers to think there's something wrong with it. So for a developer this is a careful balancing act that needs to be done properly.

Subscription service

Some games are paid for regularly on a subscription basis. The subscription service model is not a popular payment system among consumers, at least psychologically. However, it has been used widely with multiplayer games. Here, players connect via the Internet to the developer's server which contains a game world for players to exist in. Gamers are required to pay a nominal fee regularly, on a monthly or quarterly basis, to continue playing.

Episodic content

Episode games answer a number of problems both developers and players face with online downloadable games. First, consumers expect to pay less for downloadable games because the developer does not incur distribution costs, for packaging and media, etc. Also, developers want to find a means of releasing games more quickly, with a more regular and assured income rather than spending, say, years making a large downloadable game. File size is therefore an important factor. Since connections vary, gamers download the game at different speeds. Inevitably those with slower connections are less inclined to download larger games. Episode games attempt to solve this. Developers release the game in episodes – small portions – like the episodes of a soap opera. Often, episodes are left on cliff hangers which continue on in the next episode. Using this mechanism means developers can release episodes and begin developing the next. The download is smaller and the episodes are naturally cheaper than a full size game.

This book has tried to demonstrate how games are made. It is, of course, too small a book to cover every aspect of games programming. Specifically, 3D games were missing. 2D games are a good starting point for learning, but 3D games are one of the next steps. In addition to 3D games, a solid grounding in mathematics is also important, particularly in mechanics.

The best way to proceed now is to go back through this book and practise tweaking Sokoban and Hex. These are far from perfect, and could do with some cosmetic lifts. Sokoban could use some more levels, perhaps some extra tiles and some gameplay tweaks. The Hex AI also needs improving to provide a greater challenge to the player. After having played around with these projects it would be useful to create some of your own. Beyond this, the next stage of your learning will probably feature maths, physics and 3D games. For maths and physics, there are plenty of online resources, and other titles in the *Teach Yourself* series. There are in-depth resources available for making 3D games, and a good place to start with this subject would be to visit **http://www.ogre3d.org**. This is a free, open source 3D engine designed for making games.

Games programming is an exciting hobby and profession. It requires skill, dedication and a certain degree of enthusiasm. I think one of the most important things to remember is not to be dissuaded. The first few games I ever made were less than brilliant, to put it politely. But the best thing was that I learned from them, then applied my new-found knowledge in my next batch of games. Don't be disheartened if things don't always work as planned – they often don't. What is important is how you handle those situations. Some just give up; some, however, find ways around problems and keep going. Games programming will pose all sorts of problems and the easiest way to tackle them is to adopt the latter attitude. I hope this book has been informative. Enjoy the world of games!

References

Graphics resources – 2D photo editing

GIMP   http://www.gimp.org/
Adobe Photoshop   http://www.adobe.com/
Paint Shop Pro   http://www.corel.com/

Graphics resources – 3D

Blender 3D   http://www.blender.org/
MilkShape   http://chumbalum.swissquake.ch/
3D Studio Max   http://www.autodesk.com

IDE resources

Code::Blocks   http://www.codeblocks.org/
Dev C++   http://www.bloodshed.net/devcpp.html
Visual C++   http://msdn2.microsoft.com/en-us/visualc

Game libraries

SDL   http://www.libsdl.org/
DirectX   http://www.microsoft.com/windows/directx
OpenGL   http://www.opengl.org/
ClanLib   http://www.clanlib.org/
OGRE 3D   http://www.ogre3d.org/
Torque   http://www.garagegames.com/

Sound libraries

BASS Audio   http://www.un4seen.com/
FMOD   http://www.fmod.org/
OpenAL   http://www.openal.org/

Misc links

My website   http://www.alanthorn.net
Game development   http://www.gamedev.net/
Emulation and retro   http://www.theoldcomputer.com/
Independent games   http://www.gametunnel.com/
Game news and reviews   http://www.ign.com

index